Steps in history 2

L. F. Hobley

Hutchinson

London   Melbourne   Sydney   Auckland   Johannesburg

Preface

STEPS IN HISTORY is a narrative course in world history for pupils of eleven to fourteen years old. It aims to combine the recreation of historical events with an analysis of the evidence those ages have left behind them.

The first two pages of each topic offer a narrative of events; the second two pages develop the pupil's understanding of the narrative through a developing sequence of questions.

Questions 1–5 are of the same kind for each topic. They offer the simplest kind of comprehension, from which pupils can begin to familiarize themselves with names and basic facts from the text. Questions 3–5 can lead to interesting oral discussion, when pupils can follow up and justify their own written assessment of the relative importance of the given facts.

The later questions are designed to develop the pupil's ability to evaluate evidence, to reason about events, to gain a sense of time sequence, and to take an interest in the influence of events in the past upon the world today. Many of these questions will provide subjects for group and class discussion, while others will encourage pupils to write imaginatively about various subjects and situations.

Acknowledgements

Photographs

Batsford Books for p. 18; Bayerische Museum for p. 39; Bodleian Library, Oxford for p. 30; Museum Boymans–van Beuningen, Rotterdam for p. 64; The British Museum, London for pp. 7, 27 *right*, 29 *left*, 35, 43, 52, 83, 85 *right*; John Cleare/Mountain Camera for p. 59 *bottom*; Cooper Bridgeman Colour Library for p. 24; Corpus Christi College, Cambridge for p. 17; C. M. Dixon for pp. 8, 69, 73; Douglas Dickins for pp. 47, 59 *top*; D'Otrange Mastai Collection, New York: from *The Stars and the Stripes* publishers Knopf p. 95; Fotomas for p. 16; Giraudon for pp. 34, 36; Michael Holford for pp. 8, 9, 28 *bottom*; IKON for pp. 14, 19, 22, 27 *left and bottom*, 28 *centre*, 29 *left*, 34 *bottom*, 35, 36, 39, 42, 43 *bottom*, 45, 49, 53, 60, 64, 66 *bottom*, 75, 85, 89 *bottom*, 93; Arthur Lockwood for pp. 9, 12, 13, 15, 17, 25, 26, 27 *right*, 29 *centre*, 31, 32, 63 *top*, 68, 70, 83; Mansell Collection for pp. 22, 72, 76, 79 *top*, 86, 87 *top*, 90; Roland & Sabrina Michaud (John Hillelson Agency Ltd) for p. 21; National Portrait Gallery for pp. 77, 79 *bottom*, 84, 85 *centre*; Rijksmuseum, Amsterdam for p. 66 *top*; the Science Museum for p. 54; Stedelijk Museum for p. 75; Tower of London for p. 37; Trinity College, Cambridge for pp. 25, 29; Victoria & Albert Museum for p. 49; The Warburg Institute for p. 42; Werner Forman Archive for pp. 51, 67, 89 *top*; Robert Wheeler for p. 81; Windsor Castle: By Courtesy of Her Majesty the Queen, p. 63.

Illustrations

Peter Dennis for p. 80; Illustra Design Limited for pp. 6, 11, 15, 18, 23, 28, 29, 33, 44, 45, 56, 57, 62, 64, 94; Katy Pollock for pp. 10, 11, 34, 60, 61; Kathleen King for all the maps.

Hutchinson and Co. (Publishers) Ltd

An imprint of the Hutchinson Publishing Group
17–21 Conway Street, London W1P 6JD

Hutchinson Group (Australia) Pty Ltd
30–32 Cremorne Street, Richmond South, Victoria 3121
PO Box 151, Broadway, New South Wales 2007

Hutchinson Group (NZ) Ltd
32–34 View Road, PO Box 40-086, Glenfield, Auckland 10

Hutchinson Group (SA) (Pty) Ltd
PO Box 337, Bergvlei 2012, South Africa

First published 1982
© L. F. Hobley 1982

Set in Baskerville and Univers

Printed in Great Britain by The Anchor Press Ltd
and bound by Wm Brendon & Son Ltd,
both of Tiptree, Essex

British Library Cataloguing in Publication Data

Hobley, L. F.
  Steps in history
  2
  1. World history
  I. Title
  909   D21
  ISBN 0 09 148991 1

Design: Robert Wheeler
Picture Research: Christine Vincent
Additional material: James M. Hagerty

Contents

1 The geography behind history: the Old World and the New

This book tells how civilization began to develop faster again in the countries of western Europe. It tells how Europeans contacted other civilized peoples, and explored the great oceans as far as America, the New World as they called it.

A little-known world

In the early Middle Ages the people of western Europe knew scarcely anything certain about the rest of the world. A little was known of south-west Asia and of north Africa. Vague stories were told of distant India, and still more distant Cathay (China). But of America, Australia, Antarctica and of the vast Atlantic Ocean and the still vaster Pacific they knew nothing.

The Christian world map

People had no true idea of the shape or size of the earth. When they drew maps, they did not attempt to make the countries either the right shape or the correct size. The Christians regarded Jerusalem as the Holy City, and placed it in the centre of the world. Palestine, the Holy Land, was made much larger than other countries which were really far bigger.

The Moslem world map

The Moslems, whose empire covered Spain, north Africa and western Asia, were making much more accurate maps of the world, for they were more expert at sailing, measuring and mathematics. They too thought of their Holy City as being the centre of the world, but this time it was Mecca, not Jerusalem. The Crusades, which brought the Christian Europeans into contact with the civi-

The world in the Middle Ages.

lized Arab Moslem world, led to a great increase in trade, and to mark the trade routes much better maps, called *portolani*, were made of particular districts.

In the thirteenth century several journeys were made from Europe through central Asia, and Marco Polo reached the Pacific shores of China and sailed back from there to the Persian Gulf.

Columbus thought that by sailing west he would reach the Spice Islands. You can see by the dotted line how much further he would have to travel.

North Pole

East Indies

West Indies

Equator

Iceland

Scandinavia

Britain

Sweden

Russia

•Moscow

ASIA

London

Germany

Holland

EUROPE

NOMADS

• Karakorum

France

Venice

Silk route

Peking•

Portugal

Spain

Italy

Constantinople

China

Japan

TURKS

CHINESE CULTURE

Mediterranean

Palestine

Persia

PACIFIC

Jerusalem

OCEAN

Ghana

•Mecca

India

Timbuktu

Arabia

HINDU STATES

Nile

AFRICA

ABYSSINIANS

INDIAN OCEAN

Equator

AREAS OF

BLACK AFRICAN

SOCIETIES

East Indies

(Spice Islands)

Christians

Cape of Good Hope

Moslems

The round world

In the fifteenth century the period we know as the Middle Ages was coming to an end, and the explorations of the modern age were really beginning. The Portuguese were exploring the west coast of Africa, and had passed round the Cape of Good Hope to India, and some people were beginning to wonder what lay beyond the Atlantic Ocean. By that time most educated western Europeans believed that the world was round, but they did not know how large it was. Most of them followed the ideas of the ancient Greek Ptolemy, who thought it was a good deal smaller than it really is.

The first explorers who sailed westwards across the Atlantic thought that a voyage of five or six thousand kilometres would bring them to Japan, China and the Spice Islands or Indies. These are now called the East Indies, and form part of Indonesia. When Columbus, in 1492, reached the islands off the coast of America he thought they must be near India, and he called them the Indies. His mistake is remembered in the name of West Indies, which we still give them today, and in the name American Indians, given to the people whom the explorers found living in America. You will see from the map how much further away the real Indies were. In the same way when Cabot reached Newfoundland, he thought it was Japan.

Exercises and things to do

1 Write out, filling in the blanks. One – stands for each missing letter.

For some time after AD 1000, the people of western Europe knew very little about the south-west part of – – – – and scarcely anything about the countries of – – – – – and – – – – – still further east. They had no idea that the continent of – – – – – – – existed across the – – – – – – – Ocean, and they did not know whether the south of Africa was joined to – – – –. They thought the earth was – – – –, and they had no idea of its – – – –. Christians thought that – – – – – – – – was the centre of the world, and the maps of the – – – – – – – showed – – – – – as the centre. During the – – – – – – – – the Christians learned much from the – – – – – – –.

During the – – – – – – – – – – century Marco – – – – journeyed from Europe through central – – – – and reached the country of – – – – – and the – – – – – – – Ocean. The – – – – – – – – – – sailed round Africa to – – – – – and the – – – – Indies. In the year – – – – the Atlantic was crossed by – – – – – – – –.

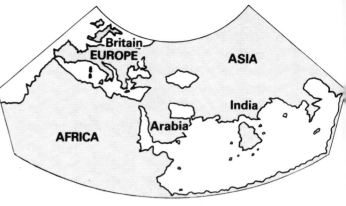

A world map drawn by Ptolemy who lived about AD 150.

2 The heads and tails of these statements have been mixed. Write them out correctly.

(a) The Portuguese	(1) thought Mecca was the centre of the world.
(b) Columbus	(2) lived in ancient Greece.
(c) The American Indians	(3) found a sea route to India.
(d) Ptolemy	(4) thought he had found a sea route to the Indies.
(e) The Moslems	(5) were named after the Indies in Asia.

3 *Statements of fact*. Write out the four statements in each group, in what you think is their order of importance or interest. Say in each group why you have decided to put one particular statement first.

(a) In the Middle Ages at first people of western Europe
  (1) knew very little about the rest of the world.
  (2) thought the earth was flat.
  (3) had no idea how big the earth was.
  (4) knew nothing of the Pacific Ocean.

(b) The Atlantic Ocean
  (1) lies to the west of Europe.
  (2) is wider between Europe and North America than between Africa and South America.
  (3) lies between America on one side and Europe and Africa on the other.
  (4) stretches both north and south of the Equator.

(c) The West Indies
  (1) lie to the north of South America.
  (2) are near Mexico.
  (3) are the largest islands between Europe and America.
  (4) are further north than the East Indies.

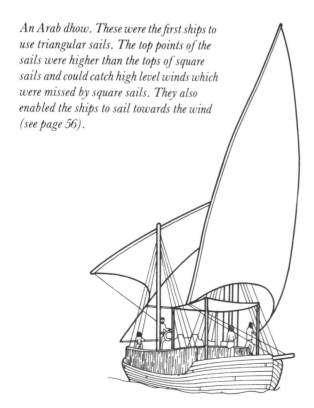

An Arab dhow. These were the first ships to use triangular sails. The top points of the sails were higher than the tops of square sails and could catch high level winds which were missed by square sails. They also enabled the ships to sail towards the wind (see page 56).

Arab world map drawn in AD 1154.

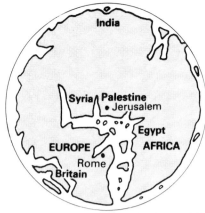

The Hereford map which was drawn in the year AD 1280. This map was drawn by Christians, who have put the Holy Land at the centre.

4 *The right order.* Arrange these places or distances in order of size, largest first.

(a) Indian, Atlantic.
(b) England to Newfoundland, Spain to Panama.
(c) London to Venice, Venice to Jerusalem, Venice to Peking.
(d) Britain to Newfoundland, Britain to Cape of Good Hope, Britain to Panama.

5 *The main idea.* Write down the one sentence which tells what you think is the main idea of this topic.

(a) Maps in the Middle Ages were not at all accurate.
(b) By the fifteenth century most educated people thought the earth was round.
(c) The growing knowledge of the world led to much better map making.
(d) As more of the world was explored, the position of western European countries became better for trade.

6 Trace the map of the world and colour or shade Mexico, Peru, East Indies, West Indies, Panama, France, Spain, Germany, Italy, Turkey, India, China, Arabia, Japan, Newfoundland, Russia, Persia.

7 Arrange these in order from north to south: Amazon, Panama, Mexico, Newfoundland, Peru.

8 Arrange these in order from west to east: Constantinople, Timbuktu, Peking, Karakorum, Venice.

9 Arrange these in order from west to east: India, Persia, Italy, Japan, China.

10 Look at the three maps above and compare them with the map on pages 4–5.

(a) Which of the three maps is the most accurate? Can you think of any reasons why?
(b) Think of as many reasons as you can why the map on pages 4–5 is more accurate than the three above.

11 Look at the picture of the Arab travellers.

(a) How are they travelling?
(b) Why do you think they chose the animals they are using?
(c) What have they done to make travel by camel more comfortable?
(d) Using the map on pages 4–5, work out where Mecca would be on the Arab map above.

A painting of a group of Arab travellers making a pilgrimage to Mecca, from a manuscript of 1566. The Arabs were great travellers and widened their knowledge of other lands.

2 The Normans

You may remember the waves of invasions by the 'Northmen' from Scandinavia. By the eleventh century most of them in their homelands and in the areas they had conquered had become Christian, but they continued to look for other lands for settlement. Two Normans, Robert Guiscard and his brother Roger, went to southern Italy to seek their fortune. Sicily had been conquered by the Arab Moslems, and the Pope made Robert Duke of southern Italy and Sicily, hoping that the Normans would take the island from the Arabs and so make it Christian again. After many years of fighting, the Arabs at least agreed to obey Duke Robert, and pay taxes to him. He then left them to keep their own religion, and follow their own laws, while he went off to attack the eastern Roman Empire; but he was killed in battle.

Meanwhile Roger Guiscard stayed in Sicily, where he built up a strong and prosperous kingdom, in which Normans, Arabs and Greeks lived and worked together in peace. When he died in 1101 his son Roger made himself king. He welcomed Arab and Greek scientists and writers to his court. One of them, the Arab Al-Idrisi, wrote a book called King Roger's Book, which contained all the knowledge about geography that had been obtained up to that time. Christian scholars in Sicily passed on a great deal of knowledge to England and France.

Stone carvings of Norman soldiers in the cathedral of Monreale, Sicily. Note their swords, shields and helmets.

William gives arms to Harold: The Bayeux Tapestry is a 70 metre long piece of needlework recording the Norman invasion of England. It was woven after the Norman Conquest. In this panel William gives weapons to Harold. William claimed that Harold would help him to become king of England.

The Normans invade England

The Normans were also attracted to another island. Edward the Confessor, the Saxon king of England, died in 1066, and William, the Duke of Normandy, claimed that Edward had promised him the throne of England. The Witan, the meeting of England's leading men, however asked the English noble, Harold, Earl of Wessex, to become king. He was crowned, and then prepared to meet an invasion by William in the south.

Suddenly news came of another Norman king who also had his eye on the English kingdom. Harold Hardrada, King of Norway, had landed in the north of England. King Harold of England hurried northwards, leaving London and the south undefended. He met Hardrada at the battle of Stamford Bridge, where he defeated and killed him. There were no more threats from the north.

The Battle of Hastings

Almost at once the news reached him that William had landed at Pevensey in Sussex. Harold marched his army quickly south again, and met William at Senlac Hill, near Hastings. In the battle which followed, Harold was killed and the English were defeated. William was crowned King of England in Westminster Abbey on Christmas Day, 1066.

King William makes sure

William made sure that the Saxons would not rise against him. All the men who fought against him had their land taken from them, and their right to keep a body of armed men-servants was abolished. In parts of England where the people did not give in at once, William slaughtered them by hun-

Provisioning the fleet: When Harold had been made king, William decided to invade England. He gathered support and sailed fo fight Harold. Here you can see his men loading the ships.

The Normans attack the English: The Normans landed at Pevensey and fought the Saxons at Senlac Hill near Hastings. In this panel you can see the Norman cavalry attacking the Saxons. Dead men lie around. William won the battle, Harold was killed, and England had a new king.

dreds, men, women and children, and burned their towns and villages. One final stand was made by the Saxons in the waterways and marshy wastes of the fens. Hereward the Wake, the Last of the English, was their leader. The Normans floundered in the muddy ooze and drowned in the black waters of the dykes. The English set fire to the reeds, and hundreds of Normans were drowned as they tried to escape from the fire. Slowly and steadily William drove a causeway through the marshes, and the last resistance was broken.

When he had made sure of his position as king, William drew up a number of laws, and saw that they were obeyed. Norman barons and Saxon serfs were all forced to keep the laws, some of which were very harsh, especially those to protect the king's deer, for he was very fond of hunting. As time passed, although the people were heavily taxed, and had to work very hard, many of them felt it was worth while, if it meant that the land was kept peaceful.

To make sure that he obtained the right amount of tax from everybody William had a great 'tax index' compiled, called the Domesday Book. Every town, village and farm was visited by the king's men, and the number of people, cattle, sheep, oxen, ploughs, mills, fishponds – everything – was written down. It was 750 years before another such survey was made. Nowadays a census is made every ten years.

Thanes and villeins

There had been many social changes since the first small Anglo-Saxon settlements, where all the villagers had fairly equal shares in the fields. The Saxon kings had appointed men called thanes to be in charge of each district, and they and their soldiers had had to be kept and supplied by the rest of the people.

Some villagers had now become more important than others, and had larger shares in the fields, and were regarded as free. They usually served the thane as soldiers when required. Most of the people of the village were known as villeins, and had from ten to thirty of the long narrow strips for their own use. Besides cultivating their own strips, they had to work for two or three days a week for the thane on his land, and also provide him with food and other services. They had to work very hard. Men, women and children all worked in the fields.

Some people, known as cottars, had little plots of land outside the big fields of strips. Some of them were craftworkers – smiths, carpenters and so on – who were expected to work part of the time for the thane, and supply him with some of the things they made.

Lower Ditchford in Gloucestershire: evidence of strip farming, old paths and the site of the village can be seen.

Exercises and things to do

1 Write out, filling in the blanks. One – stands for each missing letter.

The Northmen or Normans settled in several parts of −−−−−−, including southern −−−−− and the island of −−−−−−. Roger Guiscard became King of Sicily in AD −−−−. He had at his court −−−− and −−−−− writers.

    William, Duke of −−−−−−−−, claimed the throne of England. He defeated the English King −−−−−− at the Battle of −−−−−−−−, in AD −−−−, and was crowned −−−−.

2 The heads and tails of these statements have been mixed. Write them out correctly.

(a) Roger Guiscard	(1) was a Norman leader who became King of England.
(b) Edward the Confessor	(2) was a villager who had a few strips in the fields.
(c) A thane	(3) promised William the throne of England.
(d) A villein	(4) was a person in charge of a district of England.
(e) William the Conqueror	(5) was a Norman leader who became ruler of Sicily.

3 *Statements of fact.* Write out the four statements in each group in what you think is their order of importance or interest. Say in each case why you have decided to put one particular statement first.

(a) The English lost the Battle of Hastings
    (1) after a day of fierce fighting.
    (2) because Harold's army had recently fought a battle and made a long march.
    (3) because their men were armed with shields and axes to fight against horsemen.
    (4) because after their king was killed they gave up the struggle.

(b) William the Conqueror
    (1) was Duke of Normandy.
    (2) claimed that King Edward had promised him the throne of England.
    (3) invaded England to enforce his claim to the throne.
    (4) had the Domesday Book compiled.

(c) As King of England, William
    (1) slaughtered any Saxons who did not give in to him.
    (2) took the land from the thanes and shared it out among his followers.
    (3) crushed Saxon resistance and gave land to Norman barons and lords of the manor.
    (4) reserved for himself the best hunting land.

4 *The right order.* Write these down in the order in which they happened.
(a) The Battle of Hastings.
(b) The making of the Domesday Book.
(c) The Battle of Stamford Bridge.
(d) The crowning of William I.
(e) The crowning of Harold of England.

5 *The main idea.* Write down the one sentence which tells what you think is the main idea of this topic.

(a) The invasion of England by William brought harsh Norman rule to the English.
(b) The Norman kingdom in Sicily was prosperous, with many writers and scholars.
(c) The Normans set up several successful kingdoms.
(d) Harold was killed at the Battle of Hastings and William the Conqueror became king.

6 Look at the pictures of the Bayeux Tapestry on pages 8–9. Describe what you can see in each panel. Draw another picture for the Bayeux Tapestry showing William being crowned and surrounded by his soldiers.

A Norman banquet. The Normans spoke French, and so when an animal was killed and served up to them for a meal, it was called by the French name; but the Saxon serf, who tended the live animal, used the Saxon name, so beef (French bœuf) is the name of the meat, and ox is the Saxon name of the animal. What other examples of this use of names can you think of?

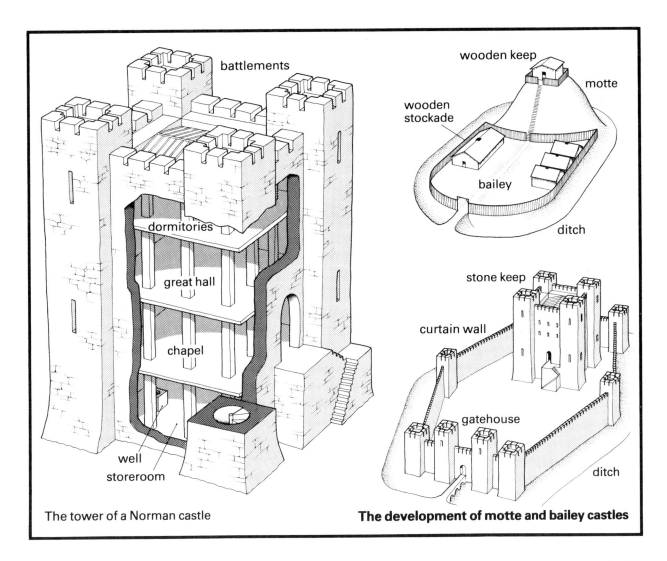

The tower of a Norman castle

The development of motte and bailey castles

7 (a) Why did William build castles?

(b) Make a list of the differences between a motte and bailey castle and later Norman castles. (Clues: wood, stone; keep, tower, stockade, wall)

8 Look at the picture of the deserted village.

(a) Draw a simple plan showing strips, paths, hedges and village.

(b) Do you think that strip farming was a good or a bad idea? Give reasons for your answers.

Building a motte and bailey castle

9 This is the sort of entry you would find in the Domesday Book.

There are 10 hides [a hide was about 48 hectares]. On the demesne [the manor lands] are 3 ploughs, 36 villeins and 12 cottars. There are 3 bailiffs. There are 2 ploughs among the men. There are 10 beasts [cattle] and 60 sheep. There are 10 hectares of meadow, and wood for 200 swine, a mill worth 12 shillings [about 60 modern pence, but a penny then would buy more than a pound would buy today], and 3 saltpans.

Write out some of the entries you think would have to be put in a Domesday Book if it were being written today about your town or village.

10 Imagine you are a Norman soldier. Write a letter to your mother telling her about your sea crossing to England, The Battle of Hastings, William being crowned and your first impressions of England and the Saxons.

January: ploughing.

3 The life of the people: masters, serfs and monks

The system of government which had grown up under the Saxon kings was continued under the Normans, but the work was often harder, and the Norman masters stricter. Each village was now known as a manor, and the man who ruled over it was called the lord of the manor. King William said that all the land belonged to him. He kept certain parts for himself, particularly areas such as the New Forest, which were good for hunting. The rest was divided between his followers, who were called tenants-in-chief. 'Tenant' means 'holder', and they did not own the land, but held it from the king on his behalf.

Nearly all the Saxon thanes lost their important positions, and were replaced by Norman barons and lords. The chief of these built castles, from which they could rule over the Saxons. Other lords of the manor built manor houses, often protected by a moat.

Lords of the manor and serfs

The lord of the manor controlled the life of all the people in the manor. Most of these were now called serfs, and they had to stay on their lord's manor, whether they wished to do so or not. A father could not let his daughter marry without the lord's permission, and if he did obtain consent, he had to make a payment to the lord.

The lord's bailiff arranged all the work of the manor, and gave his orders to the serfs every day, telling them exactly what work they were to do. If a serf was thought to have done something wrong, the lord of the manor acted as judge, so he was not likely to get much sympathy or justice if he dared

to complain against the bailiff. The life of the serfs in Norman times was hard indeed, and not only in England. One of the popes said: 'The serf serves; he is terrified with threats, wearied with forced labour, afflicted with blows, deprived of his possessions: if the lord is at fault, the serf is punished; if the serf is at fault, it is an excuse for the lord to take from him anything that he has.'

The life of the monks

Over most of Europe nine hundred years ago there were scarcely any hospitals, schools or inns. If you were ill, you hoped that the monks from the monastery would look after you. If you were travelling, you would expect to get supper and bed at a monastery. If you wanted to send your son to school, you would send him to a monastery to be taught by the monks. If you were starving, you would go to the monastery for food.

The monks were religious men who did not want to spend their lives having a home and family of their own. They thought of all men as brothers, and they devoted their whole lives to praising and worshipping God, and to helping those in need. When becoming a monk, a man gave up everything he owned, and solemnly promised not to marry, but to give all his life to what he believed to be the service of God, and always to obey the leaders of the Christian Church.

The monks lived together in a monastery, the chief part of which was the church. Near it were the cloisters, covered walks in a large square. In one part of the cloisters some of the monks taught the boys of the more important people in the

August: harvesting.

March: breaking soil, digging, sowing, harrowing.

In the Middle Ages there were two systems of farming – the open field system (three large fields divided into strips) and the closed field system (where one farmer had a number of small fields). The farmer's year was broken up by jobs such as ploughing, sowing seed, harvesting and threshing. This eleventh century calendar shows farmers at work.

neighbourhood. In another part, monks sat patiently writing copies of books with quill pens made of goose feathers, for there was no printing in those days; they had to make their own ink and colours. Others made sandals or worked at other crafts for the use of the community.

The monks lived very simply. Their food was plain and scanty. They wore sandals, and clothes of rough cloth. They slept in long bare rooms called dormitories. At midnight they got up and went into the cold church to pray. Seven more services were held in the church every day.

Out in the fields around the monastery other men called lay brothers grew crops, bred fish in the ponds, and reared sheep, cattle and pigs. The lay brothers did not lead so strict a life as the monks.

The head of the monastery was an abbot or prior, and he was a very important person. In Britain, some abbots were members of the king's

This fourteenth century monk had the keys to the wine cellar. He is taking a drink and hoping that no-one will notice.

Great Council, which helped the king in problems of government. Wealthy people sometimes left land to the monasteries when they died, so in time some monasteries became rich. Then the monks sometimes forgot the simple life they were supposed to lead, and began to enjoy comfort, feasting and merriment. They no longer worried about feeding the poor or looking after the sick.

Nuns

The work of the monks in helping others appealed to many women. Although they were not allowed to become priests or bishops, they were able to join together, and, like the monks, give themselves to the service of God and of those in need. They were called nuns, and lived in a nunnery or convent.

Some of these were for women who made vows that they would give up all contact with the rest of the world, and live entirely within the nunnery. In the early Middle Ages theirs was a life of prayer and worship, with a little time given to reading, spinning and weaving. Other nuns, often known as sisters, made simpler vows, and spent much more of their time in the nunnery on active work.

The head of a nunnery was known as an abbess or prioress, and was often a member of one of the most important families in the land. The girls of these families very often lived in a nunnery for some years until they were old enough for marriage, but some stayed on and became nuns.

In the thirteenth century other women, under the leadership of St Clare of Assisi, formed groups to live, not in nunneries, but among the people, helping those in need. They were known as Poor Clares. By the sixteenth century a number of sisterhoods had been founded, and the sisters went out into the community, nursing, teaching and acting as missionaries. Some of these, the Sisters of Charity, worked outside the convents, tending the sick and the old.

December: threshing, winnowing.

Exercises and things to do

1 Write out the following, filling in the blanks. One – stands for each missing letter.

In the Middle Ages the monks in the –––––––––– did work which today would be done by t–––––––, d–––––– and keepers of –––– and ––––––. They also looked after the very –––– when they were in ––––.

The monks worked in the ––––––––– where they –––––– books and made s–––––– and other useful things. The ––– –––––––– worked in the fields to raise the –––– for the monastery.

2 The heads and tails of these definitions have been mixed. Write them out correctly.

(a) lay brother   (1) somebody who lives in a convent

(b) monk   (2) The monks' sleeping quarters

(c) cloister   (3) a women's monastery

(d) dormitory   (4) The covered walks in a monastery

(e) prior   (5) a worker in a monastery who did not live as strictly as the monks

(f) convent   (6) head of a monastery

(g) nun   (7) a person living in a monastery

3 *Statements of fact.* Write out the four statements in each group in what you think is their order of importance or interest. Say in each group why you have decided to put one particular statement first.

(a) The Norman lords of the manor
  (1) built castles and manor houses.
  (2) acted as judges.
  (3) controlled almost all the life of the people of the manor.
  (4) appointed a bailiff to organize the work of the manor.

(b) Eight hundred years ago
  (1) there were very few inns and hospitals.
  (2) the monks looked after the sick.
  (3) the monasteries did the work of schools, hospitals and inns.
  (4) some monks were teachers.

(c) The monks
  (1) lived in monasteries.
  (2) went to church at midnight.
  (3) promised to obey those above them.
  (4) spent their lives in worship of God and helping the needy.

4 *The right order.* Write these down in the order in which they happened.
(a) The first monasteries in Britain were built.
(b) Some of the monks ceased to spend their lives helping the needy.
(c) Wealthy people left land to the monasteries.
(d) The monks lived a simple life.

A monk copying from a book. You can see the pen, ink bottles and other bound books. These monks were called scribes.

Dominicans   Carthusians   Cistercians   Franciscans

Friars and monks. Friars or brothers like St Francis worked among the sick and poor. The monks lived in monasteries away from most other people. The monasteries became very rich.

5 *The main idea.* Write down the one sentence which tells what you think is the main idea of this topic.

(a) The life of the ordinary people was hard, but the monks did much to help them.

(b) Serfs and monks were expected to work hard and obey their leaders.

(c) Monks and nuns gave up their lives to helping those in need.

(d) Kings, barons, lords and abbots had great power over those under them.

6 Look at the farming calendar and describe what you can see in each scene. What other jobs would a farmer have to do?

7 Copy one of the pictures from the calendar and then draw a picture showing how a modern farmer would do the same job.

8 Look at the box on allegiance. Make a list of the people in order of importance and explain why a promise of loyalty was important to a king.

9 What differences were made in the lives of the following when the Normans conquered England: (a) thanes (b) ordinary villagers (c) Saxon lords (d) serfs?

10 Imagine you have just spent your first few days in a monastery or a nunnery. Write a letter to a friend describing your impressions.

This diagram shows William's system of ruling. All the land belonged to him. He let his tenants-in-chief hold land in return for money and soldiers. The tenants-in-chief let sub-tenants hold some of their land in return for money and soldiers. The sub-tenants let villeins and cottars use some of their land in return for food, goods, work and soldiering. Everyone promised to be loyal to the person on the next step up in the system. But William was worried because the sub-tenants had promised to be loyal to the tenants-in-chief, and not directly to him. This meant that if a tenant-in-chief rebelled, his sub-tenants would join the rebellion, rather than supporting the king. So William summoned all the sub-tenants to Salisbury to promise loyalty directly to him.

A knight giving allegiance to his king.

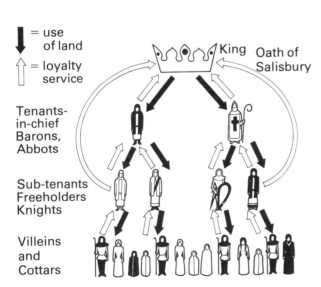

↓ = use of land
⇑ = loyalty service

King   Oath of Salisbury

Tenants-in-chief Barons, Abbots

Sub-tenants Freeholders Knights

Villeins and Cottars

4 The Crusades

Bronze model of a Crusader mounted for battle. What might he have been carrying in his right hand?

Pilgrims

Jesus Christ lived in Palestine nearly 2000 years ago. For a thousand years after that, many Christian pilgrims made the long journey from their homes in the various Christian countries to the Holy Land, as they called it, to visit the holy places connected with the life of Christ, particularly Jerusalem and Bethlehem.

Jerusalem was also one of the special holy places of the religion of Islam and its Moslem worshippers. These at first were mainly Arabs, and they allowed Christian pilgrims to visit Jerusalem, and allowed them to take charge of their holy places. But in the eleventh century there was a change. Fierce bands of Seljuk Turks rode out from the grasslands of central Asia, plundering and conquering. They seized Persia, then Syria and Palestine. By that time the Turks had adopted the Moslem religion, and in 1058 the Caliph, the head of Islam, gave the Turkish leader the title of Sultan, or leader of the Moslem world.

In 1076 the Turks captured Jerusalem. They showed none of the respect for the Christian religion which the Arabs had shown: they seized the Patriarch of Jerusalem, the Christian leader, and dragged him by the hair through the streets, and threw him into prison. They drove out the pilgrims, who fled back to their homes, telling of the cruelty of the Turks.

The conquering Turks swept on, almost to the gates of Constantinople, the centre of eastern Christianity. The emperor not only feared that the city itself might fall to the infidels, as the non-Christians were called, but he hated to see the Holy Land in the hands of the merciless Turks. He appealed to the Christians in the west for help. The Pope then urged all the Christians in western Europe to forget their quarrels and to join in a Crusade or Holy War against the Turks. Kings and nobles throughout Christian Europe began to prepare soldiers, fleets and supplies for a united attempt to seize Jerusalem from the hands of the Turks.

The First Crusade

In 1096 the armies of the First Crusade set out for Palestine. From France and Normandy, England and Flanders, Italy, Sicily and Germany they came, many under Norman leaders. By the summer of 1099 they reached Jerusalem, and after a month's siege the city was captured. The victors rode through the city, slaughtering thousands of its people, as the Turks had done to the Christians before, until the streets ran with blood. A Christian kingdom under a Norman king was set up.

After a time the Turks recovered their strength,

After his victory at Acre Richard met Saladin at the Battle of Arsuf. Here Richard (left) pulls the cross from Saladin. The dead are trampled underfoot.

and attacked the Christian kingdom. The Second Crusade was started, but the great crusading armies melted away under the Moslem attacks while disease and starvation killed them off in hundreds. The Turks then united under a great leader named Saladin, and began a Holy War too, and in 1187 they retook Jerusalem.

King Richard the Lionheart of England, King Philip of France and the Emperor Frederick of Germany united in a Third Crusade to regain the Holy City. They failed, and Jerusalem remained in Moslem hands for more than seven hundred years. But Saladin agreed to let Christian pilgrims go freely to the Holy City.

The Children's Crusade

Fighting continued, and there were several more Crusades. There was even a Children's Crusade in 1212, when thousands of children set off. Surely, people thought, God would deliver Jerusalem into the hands of innocent little children. But those who were not killed on the way were sold as slaves to the very Seljuks who were their enemy.

The last Crusades were complete failures, and in 1291 the Christians lost the last remnant of Palestine. The Turks had extended their conquests, and were stronger than ever. Two centuries of crusading had ended in almost complete failure. They may have hindered the Moslem tide of conquest, and perhaps kept Constantinople Christian for a time, but the Turks were still pressing on into eastern Europe, and in 1453 Constantinople fell at last into Moslem hands.

Who gained from the Crusades?

The real gainers from the Crusades were the Italian trading cities, particularly Venice, where huge sums of money were made by supplying ships and provisions for the crusaders, while a rich trade with the east was built up.

The Crusades were also useful to England, France and other western countries, as they took away many of the more warlike barons, and gave them plenty of fighting on foreign soil. Another benefit was that kings and barons often wanted large sums of money to pay for their crusading expenses, and so they sometimes sold charters of freedom to towns; this meant the citizens were then free to govern themselves, without having to pay taxes to the lord of the manor, or work for him. Others who gained from the Crusades were the merchants. Crusaders who were lucky enough to return often brought back with them things they had looted from the Moslems. While English nobles had only known rushes strewn on mud floors, the more civilized people of the East had fine carpets. They used knives and forks, instead of fingers. Their walls were hung with silks. When the crusaders brought back these beautiful things, those at home naturally wanted more; and so merchants were encouraged to go and set up trade links for these goods. But one should not forget the savage butchery and greedy looting for which the Christians became known, in the name of their own religion against another which they would not tolerate nor try to understand.

17

Exercises and things to do

Hospitaller

Templar

Teutonic Knight

1 Write out, filling in the blanks. One – stands for each missing letter.

In the early Middle Ages many ————————— used to make the pilgrimage to —————————, the ———— City. In AD ———— the Seljuk ————— captured the city and drove out the —————————. They then threatened —————————————, and the Emperor asked the Christians of the ———— to help them against the —————————, as the non-Christians were called.

The Pope of———— called upon all the Christian leaders to wage a ———— War or Crusade, to win back the ———— Land. In AD ———— the first crusading army set out.

After many years of fighting, and several more ————————, the ——————————— were finally driven from the ———— Land.

2 The heads and tails of these statements have been mixed. Write them out correctly.

(a) Jerusalem   (1) gained a good trade from the Crusades.

(b) The First Crusade   (2) belonged to the Christian religion.

(c) The Seljuk Turks   (3) led the victorious Moslems.

(d) The crusaders   (4) belonged to the Moslem religion.

(e) The Third Crusade   (5) led to the Christian capture of Jerusalem.

(f) Saladin   (6) was led by Richard the Lionheart.

(g) Venice   (7) was the object of many pilgrimages.

A 13th Century Knight struggling to get into his long coat of chain mail (a Hauberk).

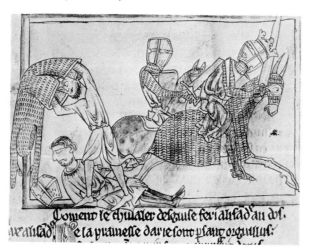

3 *Statements of fact.* Write out the four statements in each group in what you think is their order of importance or interest. Say in each group why you have decided to put one particular statement first.

(a) The Seljuk Turks
  (1) came from central Asia.
  (2) conquered Persia.
  (3) adopted the Moslem religion.
  (4) conquered Palestine and drove out the Christian pilgrims.

(b) The First Crusade
  (1) set out in AD 1096.
  (2) contained men of many countries.
  (3) sct up a Christian kingdom in Palestine.
  (4) drove the Turks from Jerusalem and slaughtered thousands of its people in 1099.

(c) The Crusades were useful to English people because they
  (1) removed warlike barons from the country.
  (2) enabled townspeople to buy charters of freedom.
  (3) spread knowledge of science and medicine.
  (4) increased trade.

4 *The right order.* Write these down in the order in which they happened.

(a) Richard the Lionheart led a Crusade.
(b) Christ was born in Palestine.
(c) The Emperor of Constantinople appealed to the West for help.
(d) The crusaders captured Jerusalem.

5 *The main idea.* Write down the one sentence which tells what you think is the main idea of this topic.

(a) The Turks captured Jerusalem and held it for centuries.
(b) The crusades were failures as Holy Wars, but they brought new ideas and trade to the West.
(c) The real gainers from the crusades were the trading cities of Italy.
(d) The Christians failed to retain Jerusalem.

6 Describe what you can see on the picture of Richard and Saladin fighting.

| Knight A | Knight B | Knight C | Knight D |

7 Copy one of the brasses or design a shield.

8 You can see the Knight struggling into his coat of mail. What other problems would a fully dressed knight have? (Clues: weight of armour; breathing)

9 Look at the brasses and complete the following chart.

During the crusades the Christian knights formed military orders dedicated to the recapture of Palestine and to the protection of pilgrims. The major orders were Knights Templar, Knights Hospitaller and Teutonic Knights. The main way of protecting a knight's body in battle was chain mail and, later armour. Here you can see brasses of medieval knights. Knights who had been on the Crusades were shown with their legs crossed over.

	Knight A	Knight B	Knight C	Knight D
Wearing chain mail				
Wearing chain mail and armour				
Wearing a helmet				
Wearing an outer garment				
Carrying a sword				
Carrying a lance				
Carrying a shield				
Wearing spurs				
Wearing elbow protection				
Wearing shoulder protection				

5 The Mongols

Stories of the East

In the Middle Ages the people of Europe knew little of the rest of the world, as they did not come into close contact with it. But they loved to hear stories of the wonders of the mysterious East, and they were always ready to believe in the existence of all sorts of strange beasts such as unicorns, and of some mythical people 'whose heads do grow beneath their shoulders'.

The East seemed to be a land of luxuries – fine silks and carpets, precious stones and spices. But the people of Europe obtained these only after the goods had made the long journey by 'caravan' of camels through central Asia or by boats like the Chinese junk or Arab dhow to the Persian Gulf or the Red Sea. By that time the goods were very expensive. The Europeans knew nothing directly of the countries from which they came.

The Mongols

Asia is a huge continent. Over its great open grassy spaces wandered the Mongol herders, tending their flocks and herds on horseback. Like the Huns, who had helped to overthrow the Roman Empire eight hundred years before, in the thirteenth century the Mongols began to conquer the countries to the east, south and west.

Under a great leader named Genghis Khan they broke through the Great Wall which had defended China for a thousand years. In AD 1214 they captured Peking and conquered most of northern China. Nearly a hundred Chinese cities were levelled to the ground, and the Mongol horsemen rode their horses over the ruins in triumph. The peasants were reduced to starvation as their crops were taken to feed the Mongol army.

Then Genghis turned westwards. His rapidly moving band of horsemen carried all before them. They had probably learned how to make gunpowder in China, and were the first army in the world to use fire-arms. They swept across central Asia, through Turkestan and southwards into India and Persia.

The Moslems were quarrelling with one another, and none was strong enough to stand against the Mongols. On swept Genghis, past the Aral Sea, past the Caspian, and on into Europe. Still no one could stop him. The Europeans too were divided, and quarrelling amongst themselves. The Grand Duke of Russia was captured, and the great plains of southern Russia came under Mongol control, as they pressed on into the heart of Europe.

The Mongol Empire

The empire of Genghis was by that time far larger than any previous emperor had ever ruled. His savage horsemen had been turned into a well-ordered army, and the plunderers were becoming civilized. Instead of destroying the cities he conquered, Genghis Khan had come to be interested in their manuscripts and works of art. Instead of persecuting people of other religions, he welcomed Christians, Moslems and Buddhists at his court. Merchants travelled from all corners of his vast empire which stretched for nearly ten thousand

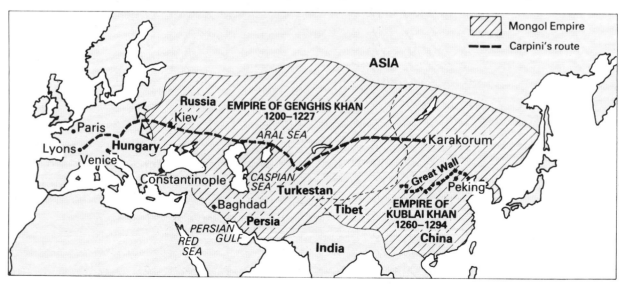

The Mongols adapted to their harsh surroundings by inventing portable homes, called yurts, which allowed them to travel to find new pastures when the old ones were exhausted. This photograph shows yurts in use in the U.S.S.R. today.

kilometres from central Europe to the Pacific. People began to wonder whether the whole world would become Mongol.

In 1227 Genghis died, but the Mongol power continued to grow. Under Ogdai Khan they pressed still further westwards. Kiev was taken and most of Russia conquered. In 1241 Polish and German armies were destroyed. Paris and London were not far away. But the forests of central Europe were not suited to the Mongol horsemen. They had no wish to conquer Paris or London, and they turned southwards into Hungary.

The next year Ogdai died, and the Mongols streamed back to the east to select a new ruler. They never penetrated so far westwards again, and their empire began to break up. In Russia the descendants of Genghis Khan formed the empire of the 'Golden Horde' and ruled the land for the next two centuries, while Kublai Khan became Emperor of China, which was for a time one of the most prosperous and civilized countries in the world.

Missionaries

The Pope of Rome, head of the Christian Church in the West, hoped that the Mongols could be persuaded to become Christian. In 1245 Pope Innocent IV sent John Carpini, a monk, and two friars with a letter to the Great Khan. Carpini set out across the plains of Tartary (southern Russia) riding on Tartar horses which, he said, 'alone could find grass under the snow, or live as animals must in Tartary, without hay or straw'. They crossed land which was 'everywhere sandie and barren, neither is the hundredth part thereof fruitefull'. There were few rivers, and the country was without villages or cities, but 'very commodious for the bringing up of cattell. I think they have more horses and mares than all the world besides.'

After many months' journey the friars reached Karakorum, the capital of Mongolia, where they marvelled at the huge quantities of silks, furs and gold. The Great Khan's tent rested on pillars of plated gold. The friars failed to convert the Khan to Christianity, but when they returned they took a friendly message from him to the Pope.

Destruction

Elsewhere, however, the Mongols continued to be terrible destroyers. In Mesopotamia (Babylonia) they utterly smashed one of the oldest civilizations. The people of Baghdad were slaughtered and their country ruined. The irrigation system which had brought prosperity for thousands of years was destroyed. The populous cities disappeared, and the fertile fields were turned into useless, unhealthy swamps or sandy wastes.

Exercises and things to do

1 Write out, filling in the blanks. One – stands for each missing letter.

The Mongols were herders who ――――――― over the vast plains of ――――, tending their flocks and ―――――. In the ――――――――― century they began conquering the countries around them. Under ――――――― ―――― they conquered much of ――――― in the east. Then they moved into ――――― and ―――――. Next they swept on half way across ―――――――. By that time Genghis Khan ruled a huge empire, and he had become more ―――――――――. He welcomed writers and people of other ――――――――― to his court.

In Babylonia (―――――――――) the Mongols destroyed the ――――――――― system, and ――――――― the country.

2 The heads and tails of these statements have been mixed. Write them out correctly.

(a) Genghis Khan	(1) made China prosperous.
(b) Ogdai Khan	(2) suffered defeat in central Europe.
(c) The Golden Horde	(3) failed to stop the Mongols.
(d) Kublai Khan	(4) was founder of the Mongol Empire.
(e) The Moslems	(5) were rulers of southern Russia.
(f) The Europeans	(6) gained a great victory in central Europe.

Kublai Khan

John Carpini

3 *Statements of fact.* Write out the four statements in each group, in what you think is their order of importance or interest. Say in each group why you have decided to put one particular statement first.

(a) The Mongols
   (1) at first lived in central Asia.
   (2) were very good horsemen.
   (3) were like the Huns.
   (4) left their homeland and conquered the surrounding peoples.

(b) Under Genghis Khan the Mongols
   (1) conquered a great empire.
   (2) broke through the Great Wall of China.
   (3) destroyed many Chinese cities.
   (4) used fire-arms.

(c) Genghis Khan succeeded because
   (1) he was a great leader.
   (2) the Moslems were quarrelling with one another.
   (3) his men used gunpowder.
   (4) the Europeans were quarrelling with one another.

4 *The right order.* Write these down in the order in which they happened.

(1) Genghis Khan conquered China.
(2) Kublai Khan ruled China.
(3) Ogdai Khan ruled the Mongols.
(4) Genghis Khan invaded Europe.
(5) The Huns attacked the Roman Empire.

5 *The main idea.* Write down the one sentence which tells what you think is the main idea of this topic.

(a) Genghis Khan led the Mongols to victory.
(b) The Pope failed to convert the Mongols to Christianity.
(c) The Mongols conquered many lands, destroying some, and ruling some well.
(d) The Mongol empire stretched from central Europe to the Pacific.

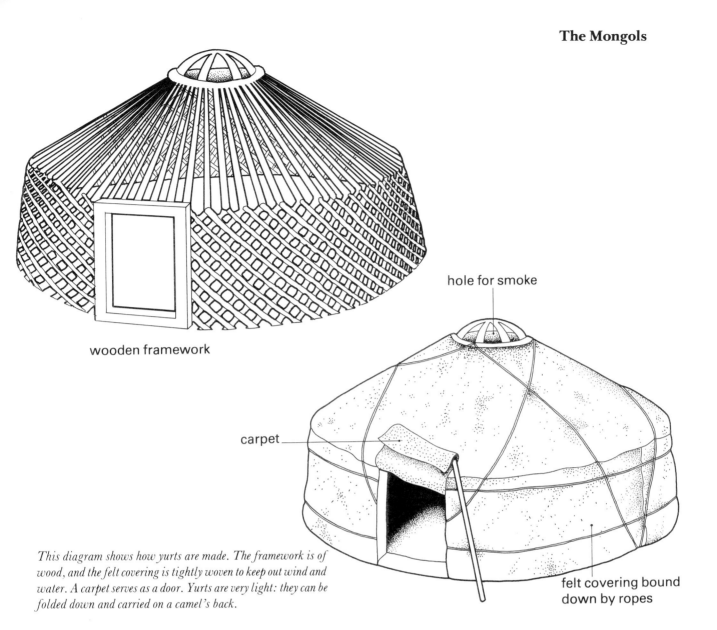

wooden framework

hole for smoke

carpet

felt covering bound
down by ropes

This diagram shows how yurts are made. The framework is of wood, and the felt covering is tightly woven to keep out wind and water. A carpet serves as a door. Yurts are very light: they can be folded down and carried on a camel's back.

6 *Thinking back.* Write out these sentences choosing the right word from the bracket, if possible without looking back at previous topics.

(a) Other peoples to come from the plains of central Asia were the (Arabs, Turks, Normans).
(b) The people of (north Africa, northern Europe, western Europe) were Moslems.
(c) The great Turkish leader in the Crusades was (Mohammed, Saladin, Richard).
(d) The greatest traders of Europe in the Middle Ages were from (Venice, Rome, Normandy).

7 Why did the Mongols build up such a huge empire so quickly? Give as many reasons as you can suggest.

8 Write an article that might have appeared in an English newspaper in 1241 (if there had been any), describing the advance of the Mongols into Europe.

9 Write the letter Pope Innocent IV might have sent to the Great Khan, and also the letter that the Khan might have sent back.

10 Who or what were the following?

(a) The capital of Mongolia
(b) A Khan
(c) The Great Khan
(d) The great thirteenth century empire
(e) The head of the Christian Church of western Europe
(f) Pope Innocent IV's messenger to the Great Khan
(g) The land which Carpini thought had more horses than all the world besides.

11 Look at the map and name four countries in the Empire of the Khans.

6 Trade and exploration

Trade and the Europeans

What does trade mean to people? If the country has not many resources of its own, it may mean all the difference between a comfortable, varied life and one of hardship and shortage of food and clothing. Britain, for example, is a small country with many people, and cannot grow enough food for all of them; so Britain now manufactures many things in factories, and trades them for food and raw materials.

After the fall of the Roman Empire, trade in Europe almost ceased, and people had to live on what they could grow themselves. There were no oranges, bananas or other fruits from warmer countries, no tea, coffee or cocoa, no chocolates, no cotton material, no silk; none of the hundreds of things from foreign countries which people have come to rely on today.

Workers pick grapes in the vineyards of a rich landowner. The wine trade became very important in mainland Europe.

Venice and China

The merchants of Venice were trying to extend their trade. About AD 1260 two merchants of Venice, Nicolo and Maffeo Polo, went on a long journey. They intended to trade with the Tartars of the Black Sea area, but the mystery of the East captivated them, and they decided to venture into the heart of the Mongol country. They were kindly treated by the Khans, and stayed with them for some time, learning the Tartar language. They were invited to go on to Peking, the Chinese capital of Kublai Khan. Kublai welcomed them, and listened with interest to all that the Venetians had to say about their own land, and the Christian religion. Then he sent them back to Italy with letters asking the Pope to send 'a hundred men learned in the Christian religion, well versed in the seven arts, and able to show that their own beliefs were the best'.

The Polos made the long journey home. The Pope was able to find only two friars to send to Kublai, so the Polos set off with them on yet another three-year journey. They took with them Nicolo's son Marco. They had not gone far when the friars grew afraid and turned back, but the Polos rode on.

China

Kublai was very pleased to see them, and delighted with the young Marco, who soon learned four of the Tartar languages and methods of writing. Marco was sent by Kublai on many journeys to different parts of China, and he wrote about the wonders he saw. In Peking, the capital city, scholars and missionaries of many religions and races exchanged ideas, and merchants from distant lands exchanged their wares. The city had vast palaces and was a great trading centre.

Return to Venice

After seventeen years in China, the Polos returned to Venice. In their travel-stained clothes, they were not recognized by their friends, who thought they were beggars; but when the Polos slit open the seams, they released a shower of rubies, diamonds and emeralds.

The Polos and other Christians failed to convert

How trade developed

Then gradually the countries of Europe became more peaceful, and the barbarians settled down. At first nearly everybody lived in little villages, but the nobles began to have castles built, kings and bishops built palaces, monasteries and churches. Materials for building, and supplies for the men employed, often had to be obtained from elsewhere, so markets were established, and trade developed. The nobles and ladies who lived in the castles wanted more and better kinds of food, furniture, clothes and other things, and this led to more trade. Market towns grew up near the castles; the craftworkers in the towns, like the nobles, needed materials to work with, and food which they had not time to grow for themselves; and the people who arranged these supplies gradually became more wealthy and important. They began to go further afield for their goods, and developed ships and trade routes.

Great traders of the Middle Ages

The great European traders of the Middle Ages were the Italians of Venice and Genoa. Ships were small, and voyages took a long time, so most of the goods carried were expensive luxuries. They came mainly from the East. The Venetians bought them from the eastern merchants and took them to the great markets of Venice. From there they were sent by land and sea to all the countries of western Europe.

England's trade

Much of England's trade in the Middle Ages was with Italy. At first most of it followed the land route across Europe, the only sea voyage being across the narrow seas between Flanders and England. Only some Venetian ships made the long voyage through the Straits of Gibraltar to England. After the Third Crusade English ships began to make the voyage to the Mediterranean.

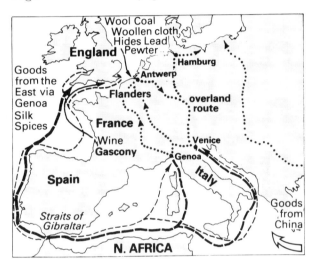

the Mongols to Christianity. The worshippers of Islam were more successful, and the Mongols became Moslems. In the fourteenth century they closed the East to all other religions.

Kublai Khan and Marco Polo using paper money. The Venetians made long journeys in an attempt to improve trade between countries. Goods, money and ideas were exchanged. Towns and trade routes developed.

Exercises and things to do

1 Write out, filling in the blanks. One – stands for each missing letter.

Trade was becoming more important in the Middle Ages. The first great trading cities were −−−−−− and −−−−− in Italy. Much of England's trade was with −−−−−. At first it followed the −−−− route, but after the −−−−− −−−−−−− England began to trade by −−−.

The desire to increase trade led to journeys to open up new −−−−− −−−−−−. Nicolo and −−−−−− −−−− travelled all the way to −−−−−−, the Chinese capital of −−−−−− −−−−, who asked them to go back and fetch some men to teach him about the −−−−−−−− religion.

2 The heads and tails of these statements have been mixed. Write them out correctly.

(a) Peking	(1) was an Italian port.
(b) Genoa	(2) was the land near the Black Sea.
(c) Silk	(3) was the main export of England.
(d) Tartary	(4) was the capital of China.
(e) Wool	(5) was an important export from China.

3 *Statements of fact.* Write out the four statements in each group in what you think is their order of importance or interest. Say in each group why you have decided to put one particular statement first.

(a) In the Middle Ages
    (1) trade grew up gradually in the towns.
    (2) towns grew up around the castles.
    (3) trade gradually became important as castles and towns brought numbers of people together.
    (4) craftworkers' need for materials helped to create trade.

(b) Britain is particularly interested in trade because
    (1) it is a small country with many people.
    (2) people in Britain cannot grow enough food for themselves.
    (3) Britain has to make and export goods in exchange for food and raw materials.
    (4) it is trade which helps to make British people prosperous.

(c) European trade in the Middle Ages
    (1) was carried on largely by Italians.
    (2) brought the luxuries of the East to western Europe.
    (3) brought great wealth to Venice.
    (4) led to the search for new sources of trade and trade routes.

The wool trade was very important in the Middle Ages. Whole families were involved in the making of cloth. Here the women spin and weave.

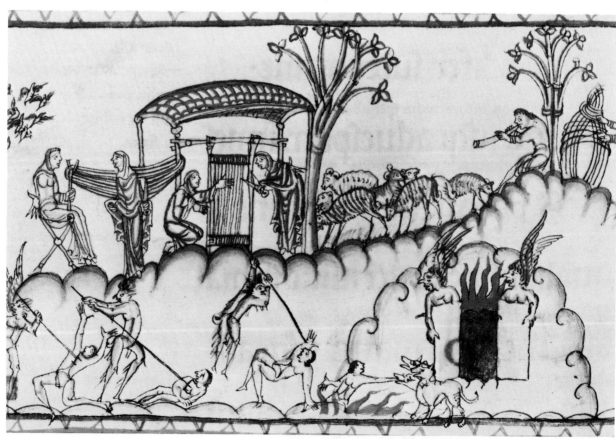

A maid helps her mistress to comb and plait her hair. She is also holding a mirror.

After plaiting their hair, ladies covered their heads with tall, peaked hats called henins.

4 *The right order.* Write these down in the order in which they happened.

(a) English ships began trading in the Mediterranean.
(b) Marco Polo made journeys for Kublai Khan.
(c) Trade in Europe practically ceased.
(d) The three Polos set out for Peking.
(e) The building of castles, towns and churches helped the growth of trade.

5 *The main idea.* Write down the one sentence which tells what you think is the main idea of this topic.

(a) European trade in the Middle Ages was mainly with the East.
(b) Luxury trade with the East through Italy increased in the Middle Ages.
(c) In the thirteenth century traders and friars from Europe visited the Mongols in China.
(d) European trade in the Middle Ages passed largely through Venice and brought it great wealth.

Rich men wore short tunics and tight fitting stockings or hose. The also wore pointed leather shoes and hats.

6 In the Middle Ages wool was the chief export from England. A merchant carved over his new house: 'I thank God and ever shall
　　　　It is the sheep hath paid for all.'
In 1300 raw wool exports amounted to 30 000 sacks. By 1450 woollen cloth had taken the place of raw wool which had fallen to 8000 sacks while export of woollen cloth had risen from 5000 bales to 54 000. Why was this, do you think? Make a diagram to show these changes.

7 Write out a list of ten countries and against each one write in one of its products. An example may be: Japan – cars.

8 Find out which countries use the following currency (money) – cents, pennies, francs, Marks, lira, roubles, peseta, yen, guilder, rupee.

9 Using other books draw three pictures to show how ladies' and men's clothing styles have changed. Write a date under each drawing.

Food and health

Cooking and flavouring herbs

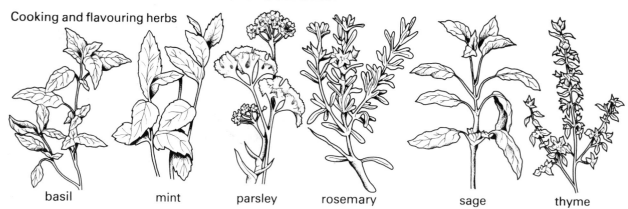

basil   mint   parsley   rosemary   sage   thyme

Before modern preserving and refrigeration methods were invented, people could eat only foods which were in season and so the variety was very limited. Herbs and spices helped to preserve and make the food more interesting. Some people also realised that herbs could be used a medicines. Spices were not grown in Europe and there was rivalry among merchants to bring them from the Far East.

A wooden carving showing a wife scolding her husband for stealing from the cooking pot. In the Middle Ages most cooking was done over an open fire.

This scene from the Bayeux Tapestry shows cooks preparing food in a big pot over an open fire. On the shelf above them there are pieces of meat on spits. To the right the baker pulls loaves of bread from an oven.

Medicinal herbs

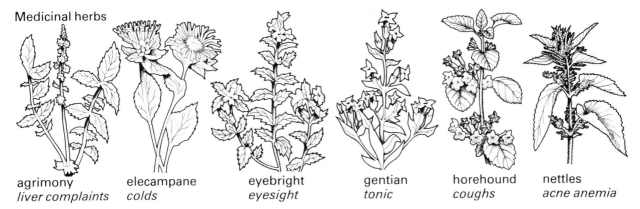

agrimony	elecampane	eyebright	gentian	horehound	nettles
liver complaints	*colds*	*eyesight*	*tonic*	*coughs*	*acne anemia*

A thirteenth-century illustration showing an operation. There was none of the hygiene, anaesthetic and medical skill that we have today. The apothecary (chemist) would prepare herbs for use as medicine. The surgeon would perform operations. Here you can see a surgeon performing an operation whilst an assistant holds the patient down and another demands payment.

Although the Church frowned upon the cutting up of corpses it was an important way for doctors to find out about disease and illness. It also led to an increased knowledge of the human body. In this fifteenth-century French illustration doctors examine a corpse.

1 What are the main differences between a medieval kitchen and a modern one?

2 How many of the herbs shown here do you have at home? Look at the labels to see what they are used for.

3 Copy and colour two of the herbs which were used as medicines.

4 What would you use as medicines instead of the herbs on this page?

5 Imagine you are the patient in the picture above. Write a letter to a friend after the operation, describing what happened and what it felt like. Make your letter as vivid as possible.

29

7 Kings, barons and people: Magna Carta, Wales and Scotland

King William

Kings and queens nowadays cannot do just as they like. In Britain the king or queen has very little power, and the country is governed by Parliament, which makes the laws and sees that people obey them. In the past, kings and queens had much more of their own way, though even William the Conqueror asked advice of a Great Council of barons, bishops and abbots. The ordinary people had no say at all in how the country was run.

King John

King John, who came to the throne in 1199, quarrelled with the King of France, was defeated and

King Henry I had a nightmare about his problems. He dreamt that labourers and priests gave him lists of complaints whilst his soldiers threatened him.

lost his land in Normandy. This annoyed many English barons who had now lost their own lands in France.

He also had to pay the Pope a large sum of money each year, and to obtain this he took property away from people who displeased him, and fined and imprisoned people without trial. He also raised heavy taxes. Nobody liked this, and all the most powerful men joined together under the leadership of Stephen Langton, Archbishop of Canterbury. There were bishops and abbots who spoke for the Church, all the leading barons, and some of the chief merchants from London and other towns. This was the first time that citizens of this kind had taken an important part in the country's affairs.

Rules for the king

They drew up a long list of sixty rules which the king would have to obey. They were set out in the Magna Carta, or Great Charter, and in 1215 it was presented to John at Runnymede. He was furious, but nearly everyone was against him, so he ordered that the royal seal should be placed upon the Charter. This meant that he promised that the Church should be free from interference, that the nobles should be tried by a jury of nobles, and not by the King's Court, that taxes should not be imposed without the consent of the Great Council, that he would not interfere with trade, that towns should keep their freedom, and that no free person should be imprisoned without trial. Twenty-five barons were appointed to see that John kept his promise.

The first Parliament

The kings and queens who ruled after John all promised to keep the Charter, but they did not always do so. There was much discontent with the next king, Henry III, and in 1264 Simon de Montfort led all those who were opposed to Henry, beat him at the battle of Lewes and took him prisoner. Simon then called a new kind of Great Council: besides the usual barons and bishops, it had knights to represent the country lords of the manor, and burgesses (citizens) to

represent the merchants of the chief towns. This was the beginning of the kind of Parliament we have today.

In 1295 King Edward I called a similar Great Council, and this was known as the Model Parliament. But it would be six hundred years before the ordinary people could be Members of Parliament, or even choose Members of Parliament by voting at elections.

The King of England and Wales

Edward I decided that he would increase his power by uniting Wales and Scotland with England under himself. William the Conqueror had given his most warlike barons estates on the Welsh border, so that they could protect the border lands from raids by the Welsh. As a result, much of Wales had been conquered during the next two hundred years, and the Welsh were driven into the north-west of their country. Here they were ruled by Prince Llewellyn, who refused to recognize King Edward as his overlord.

In 1277 Edward led an army against Llewellyn. Llewellyn was starved out, and had to give in. Edward replaced the Welsh laws with English ones. The Welsh were furious, and Llewellyn and his brother David led them in revolt. But both were killed, and the revolt came to an end. In 1284 all Wales was divided into counties in the English fashion, but the Welsh were allowed to keep some of their own laws and customs.

The Parliament of Edward I. The King of Scotland and the Prince of Wales sit beside the King of England. Archbishops, bishops, judges and other lords are also shown.

Scotland

Next Edward tried to gain control of Scotland. The Scots made a treaty with France, England's old enemy. Dover was burned by the French, and England's important wool trade with Europe was stopped. Edward made up his mind to conquer Scotland completely. In 1296 he defeated the Scots, and ruled the country as if it was a part of England. Some of the Scottish nobles had lands in England as well, and they were prepared to obey the English king, but the farmers and the ordinary Scottish people were not. The Scottish leader William Wallace gathered an army and beat the English at the battle of Stirling Bridge. Edward hurried northwards, defeated Wallace at Falkirk, and had him executed as a rebel. This only angered the Scots still more. Robert Bruce took the place of Wallace, and gradually drove the English from their castles and strong points. Once more Edward set out for the north, but on the way he died.

His son Edward II was completely defeated by Bruce at Bannockburn in 1314. The English then gave up the attempt to conquer Scotland, and for a very long time the two countries were enemies, raiding each other across the border.

Exercises and things to do

1 Write out, filling in the blanks. One – stands for each missing letter.

King John – – – – – – everybody. He lost his land in – – – – – –, which upset some of his – – – – – –, and made the people pay heavy – – –.– –. So in AD – – – – all joined together, b– – – – –, m– – – – – – – –, and leaders of the – – – – – –, to make him agree to the – – – – – – – – – – –, or – – – – – – – – – –. By this he promised to rule as the – – – – – – – – – – – – told him to. All kings since then have promised to obey the – – – – – – – – – – –.

King Edward I tried to extend his power over – – – – – and – – – – – – – –. He managed to conquer the – – – – –, but although he won several – – – – – – – against the Scots, and executed their leader, – – – – – – – – – – – – – –, they found a new leader in – – – – – – – – – – –. In AD – – – – the English were beaten at – – – – – – – – – – – and driven out of Scotland.

Medieval leisure and pleasure. Swings, puppet shows, dancing bears, acrobats, mimes, plays, music and ball games were all very popular.

2 The heads and tails of these statements have been mixed. Write them out correctly.

(a) King John	(1) led the Scots at Bannockburn.
(b) Stephen Langton	(2) defeated Henry III and called a Parliament.
(c) Simon de Montfort	(3) was forced to sign the Great Charter.
(d) Llewellyn	(4) led the barons who forced the king to sign the Great Charter.
(e) Robert Bruce	(5) was defeated by Edward I.

3 *Statements of fact.* Write out the four statements in each group in what you think is their order of importance or interest. Say in each group why you have decided to put one particular statement first.

(a) The purpose of the Great Charter was to
  (1) make the king obey the law of the land.
  (2) limit the power of the king.
  (3) prevent the king from imprisoning free men without fair trial.
  (4) prevent the king from levying taxes without the consent of the Great Council.

(b) The English Parliament
  (1) grew out of the Great Council.
  (2) included knights and burgesses after 1264.
  (3) developed out of the ideas of Simon de Montfort and Edward I in having knights and burgesses as well as barons and bishops.
  (4) shared with the king the government of England.

(c) Edward I's attempt to control Scotland
  (1) was finally unsuccessful.
  (2) united the Scottish people against him.
  (3) led to long years of enmity between England and Scotland.
  (4) failed in the end because it led nearly all the Scots to unite against the English.

4 *The right order.* Write these down in the order in which they happened.

(a) King John sealed the Magna Carta.
(b) The Battle of Bannockburn.
(c) All Wales was finally divided into counties and given English laws.
(d) Wallace led the Scots against Edward.
(e) Knights and burgesses were first included in Parliament.

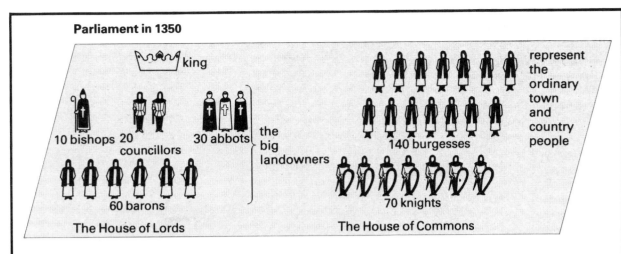

Parliament in 1350

king

10 bishops 20 councillors 30 abbots the big landowners

60 barons

The House of Lords

140 burgesses

70 knights

represent the ordinary town and country people

The House of Commons

Parliament today

300 regular attendants
[1200 members in all:
800 hereditary peers
325 life peers
26 bishops (Church of England)
11 law lords]

The House of Lords

635 members

The House of Commons

In the Middle Ages only a few people had a part in governing the country. They were usually bishops, abbots and rich landowners and merchants. However, over the centuries

Parliament has changed. The House of Lords (unelected) still remains but the House of Commons (elected) is much bigger and represents more people.

5 *The main idea.* Write down the one sentence which tells what you think is the main idea of this topic.

(a) As the Great Council developed into Parliament, the power of the king grew less.
(b) King John was unpopular with almost everyone in England.
(c) The power of the king was reduced when King John sealed the Magna Carta in 1215.
(d) The English kings increased their power over the Welsh, but not over the Scots.

6 Make up a play and act it showing King John being told about the Great Charter, and the scene where he has to seal it.

7 Act a play in which William Wallace is tried as a traitor by a London judge, and in which he makes a speech in his defence.

8 Find out the name of the Member of Parliament for your district. What sort of person is he or she: a lawyer, a tradesman, a housewife, a manual labourer, a rich land-owner, a trade union official or what? Does your local bishop sit in the House of Lords?

9 Look at the diagram of Parliament in 1350 and today. What are the main similarities? What are the main differences?

10 Make a list of medieval games and pastimes. Against this write out a list of modern games and leisure activities.

11 Using either the picture on page 32 or those in other books design a poster to advertise the coming of a medieval fun fair.

8 Trade, war, plague and revolt

In the fourteenth century trade was becoming much more important to England, particularly in wool, which was sold mainly to Flanders. This brought great profit to both nobles and the Church, for both owned many large sheep farms. The merchants who bought, transported and sold the wool were also becoming wealthy.

King Edward III's mother was French, and he already ruled large parts of France. He wanted to gain control of Flanders to protect the rich wool trade, so he claimed to be the rightful king of all France. In 1338 he started what came to be called the Hundred Years War. He invaded France and met the French at Crécy in 1346. The English army won the battle, but the war continued for more than a hundred years.

What was happening in England?

In 1349 some of the victorious soldiers returned to England. They found it a land of fear. The streets were empty and desolate. People huddled in their homes, or crept to a nearby church to beg God for mercy. Now and then a cart carried a load of corpses through the silent street to a great pit outside the town. In the villages the beasts wandered untended, the crops rotted in the fields. Bodies sometimes lay unburied. The Black Death had spread terror through all the land.

This terrible plague had started in far-off China. Ships and caravans carried the deadly infection to the West. The plague ran like wildfire through Italy and into France and Spain. In July 1348 the fatal ship that brought the Death to England sailed from France to Dorset. The plague spread. In October it reached London. Within a few days thousands of people died. The Archbishop of Canterbury went to London to bring hope to the people, but within two days he too was dead. Some people fled from the city to the woods, but the plague followed them.

Many of England's great war victories were won mainly by the bowmen. Edward stopped most games such as football and hunting with dogs, and made all men practise shooting with the long bow. It was possible to shoot an arrow nearly 600 metres, and the 'killing' distance was anything up to 250 metres. Most foreigners used the crossbow, which was much slower in use, and less deadly.

The plague was carried by fleas which lived on the bodies of rats. The fleas passed the plague to human beings who then passed it on to one another.

At last, in the autumn of 1349, the plague died down. About a third of all the people of England had died. In some places almost the whole population had been wiped out. Fields were unploughed and without crops, the hay was uncut, the animals neglected. There were not enough people to do all the necessary work, and lords of the manor were often left without any serfs to work their land. They began offering to pay wages to people from other places to come and work for them.

The Members of Parliament, who were nearly all men with wide lands needing to be worked, did not like having to pay wages, and they passed laws forbidding high wages. They also taxed all the people by a fixed amount which meant that the

The plague reached England in 1348–9. It became known as the Black Death. In England four out of every seven people died of the plague. Here the victims are buried.

poor suffered more than the rich. The peasants became more and more dissatisfied. Led by a priest named John Ball, they began to talk of the Great Society, when all should be fairly treated, and there would be no serfs and lords, but all free people.

Revolt

In 1381 John Ball and Wat Tyler led thousands of country people towards London, demanding to see the king, who, they felt sure, would see that they were fairly treated.

The fourteen-year-old King Richard II and his ministers met the peasants. There was a dispute, and Tyler was killed. The peasants shouted angrily when they saw their leader fall, but the king rode forward and cried out, 'I will be your leader,' and promised that serfdom would be ended and their demands would be granted. Satisfied with this royal promise, the peasants returned home. But when they reached their villages in widely scattered parts of the country, the soldiers followed them. Hundreds of peasants were put to death. Instead of the king's promise of freedom, they were told, 'Serfs you are, and serfs you will remain.'

This Peasants' Revolt, however, was not a complete failure. Later Parliaments no longer tried to keep wages down to the old low levels. Gradually, too, the serfs gained more freedom, and many of them became free men working for wages, or free peasant farmers with their own holdings of land.

In this scene two events are shown. Richard II talks to the rebels and then rides away. On the left Wat Tyler is killed by the Lord Mayor of London.

War continues

Meanwhile the war in France continued. In 1415 King Henry V won the Battle of Agincourt, but then a simple eighteen-year-old peasant girl changed everything. She hated the war and the suffering it brought to the ordinary people. She heard the voices of angels and saints telling her to go to the French Prince Charles, and ask him to let her lead the French army against the English at Orleans, and then go on to free Reims, the old capital of France, and have him crowned there.

At first people laughed at the idea, but there was something about Joan of Arc which convinced people. First the common soldiers, then the generals, then Charles and the archbishop, believed in her. In shining armour, she rode to Orleans which the English had been besieging for months. Within nine days the English were in retreat. The Maid of Orleans, as they called her, filled the French with fresh courage. They drove the English from Reims, and Charles was crowned there, just as Joan's voices had foretold. But then she was captured by the Burgundians, who were sympathetic to the English. She was handed over to the English, who burned her alive as a witch, but the French continued to win battles. By 1453 England had lost all France except Calais.

Exercises and things to do

1 Write out, filling in the blanks. One – stands for each missing letter.

King Edward III claimed that he ought to be king of all − − − − − −. He did this partly because he wanted to control the rich − − − − − in − − − − with − − − − − − − −. The − − − − − − − Years − − − started in − − − −.

When the English soldiers returned home after the Battle of − − − − −, they found that a terrible − − − − − −, called the − − − − − − − − − −, had killed so many of the people that there were not enough men to do the − − − − in the fields. The peasants began to feel that they deserved − − − − wages, and when − − − − − − − − − passed a − − − stopping this, they were angry, and marched on − − − − − −. After this − − − − − − − Revolt, things began to get better for the serfs and − − − − − − − −.

Meanwhile a young girl in − − − − − − had changed the course of the − − −. She led the − − − − − − army and defeated the English at − − − − − − − and − − − − −. Her name was − − − − − − − − −. The English burned her as a − − − − −, but soon they were driven out of all − − − − − − except − − − − − −.

The French prince greets Joan of Arc outside the town of Chinon (from a fifteenth century tapestry).

2 The heads and tails of these statements have been mixed. Write them out correctly.

(a) Richard II	(1) was killed in the Peasants' Revolt.
(b) The Hundred Years War	(2) was a struggle between the peasants and Parliament.
(c) John Ball	(3) was only a boy, but he quietened the peasants.
(d) The Peasants' Revolt	(4) was a long war between England and France.
(e) Wat Tyler	(5) was the priest who led the peasants.

3 *Statements of fact.* Write out the four statements in each group in what you think is their order of importance or interest. Say in each group why you have decided to put one particular statement first.

(a) As a result of the Black Death
   (1) a third of the people of England died.
   (2) the population of some villages was almost wiped out.
   (3) so many people died that work, wages and many other conditions were changed.
   (4) crops were not harvested and farm animals were neglected.

(b) The Peasants' Revolt
   (1) was an attempt by the peasants to gain a better, fairer life.
   (2) was led by Wat Tyler.
   (3) involved a great march to London by thousands of peasants.
   (4) was ended when King Richard promised the peasants what they wanted.

(c) Joan of Arc
   (1) was a simple country girl who heard voices telling her that she could save France.
   (2) persuaded the King of France to let her lead the French armies.
   (3) drove the English from Orleans and Reims.
   (4) was burned as a witch by the English.

4 *The right order.* Write these down in the order in which they happened.

(a) John Ball began to talk of the Great Society.
(b) The Battle of Crécy.
(c) The English were driven from all France except Calais.
(d) Shortage of labour led to a big rise in wages.
(e) The Black Death reached London.

5 *The main idea.* Write down the one sentence which tells what you think is the main idea of this topic.

(a) The Black Death killed so many men that the peasants realized how important they were.

(b) The Peasants' Revolt aimed at getting rid of serfdom and gaining freedom.

(c) The War and the Black Death made the ordinary men realize their importance and their strength.

(d) The Hundred Years War showed that bowmen were more effective soldiers than old-fashioned knights in armour.

6 Write a newspaper report on either the Peasants' Revolt or the plague affecting your town. (Use the pictures to help you.)

A firemaster directs a cannon attack on a castle. Crossbowmen also send flaming arrows into the castle. Defenders pull the arrows out of the roof.

7 Make a speech that a lord of the manor might have made to Parliament in favour of the Statute of Labourers, to stop the payment of higher wages.

8 Imagine you were a longbow man at Crecy. Write up your diary for the day of the battle.

9 Look at the picture of Joan of Arc arriving at Chinon. It is after Joan's victories. What might the prince say to her?

10 Study the picture of the castle being attacked. Make a list of the attackers' equipment and a list of the ways in which the castle was defended.

9 Cities of the Middle Ages: the story of Constantinople

In the Middle Ages there were many free cities in Europe. They made their own laws and tried citizens in their own town court; they built walls round the city and raised their own armies to defend themselves. In England the towns were less independent, as the king usually kept a stricter control over the whole country.

The centre of city life

In almost all cities, the church or cathedral was the most important building. Nearly all the people went to church frequently, for it was the centre of city life. As well as the regular services, it might be used as a theatre for religious plays, a meeting hall for scholars, and even as a dining hall for a great festival. The leading churchmen had hospitals built for the sick, and almshouses for the poor and old.

The other main centre was the market place. Here, besides stalls for buying and selling, the guilds of various craftworkers put up stages to perform their mystery plays. Here too, on the gallows, at the whipping post and in the stocks, criminals suffered cruel punishments.

Carcassonne, France: a walled town built in the Middle Ages which is still standing today.

The cities were not large, compared with those of today. Their streets were winding and narrow, but there was little wheeled traffic. Many cities had some public baths, and some had piped water to the main streets. Sewage was not flushed away, as it is today, but in most cities it was cleared regularly and used to increase the fertility of the surrounding farm land.

Italian cities

Some of the earliest and greatest free cities were in Italy, where Florence, Genoa, Milan and Venice became rich and powerful. They were often ruled by one or a small group of families, who vied with one another in making their city beautiful. Gradually the princes of various states absorbed the free Italian cities into their countries, and by the fifteenth century Venice was the only great independent city left in Italy.

Dutch cities

By the thirteenth century Dutch and Flemish merchants had grown rich from trading and the manufacture of cloth. They built some fine cities, such as Bruges, Ghent and Antwerp. Sometimes neighbouring cities fought one another fiercely, sometimes they combined to fight for their freedom against England or France.

This large crane was used in Flanders during the fourteenth century. The men walking on the treadwheel provided the power.

The Hanseatic cities

Throughout northern Germany and lands near the Baltic, many free cities grew up. Each had a Hanse House or Guild Hall, and when they joined together they became known as the Hanseatic League. Under the leadership of Hamburg and Lubeck they kept the seas free from pirates, and were strong enough to go to war with the kingdom of Denmark and beat her.

The Hanse towns were governed entirely by a council of merchants; neither nobles nor workmen had any influence. The council raised and trained an army, organized fire brigades, fixed the prices of goods and wages for workers, levied taxes on citizens and visitors, and made sure that the goods sold in the city were of good quality. As kings became stronger, they absorbed some of the cities. When America was discovered in the fifteenth century, and a sea route to India was found, the Baltic cities rapidly declined in power, because the north coast became less important than the west and east.

Constantinople

Greater than all the cities of the Middle Ages was Constantinople. It was not a creation of the Middle Ages, but the last of the great cities of Roman times. It was not a free city, but was itself the capital of the Eastern or Byzantine Empire. It was built by the Roman Emperor Constantine as a centre of the Roman Empire, with Roman laws, but it had Greek culture and ideas, and the Eastern or Orthodox Christian religion. When Rome fell, it remained the capital of the Byzantine Empire for another thousand years, beating back attacks from all sides.

The Great City

Constantinople was the great meeting place of routes from the east and west by land, and from north and south by sea, from the far Baltic, by the long Russian rivers, and across the Black Sea, and from the Mediterranean in the south. In the markets, merchants from the north and west met those from Africa and the East. In its shops all the luxuries of the known world were displayed. People of every race thronged its broad main streets, and crowds jostled in the steep narrow lanes leading down to the thousand ships in the harbour.

The end of the Byzantine Empire

Constantinople was a great Christian fortress in the non-Christian world. In 1071 the Moslem Seljuk Turks defeated the Byzantines, and Constantinople was in danger. The Emperor appealed to the western Christians for help, and in the Crusades the Turks were halted.

The merchants of Venice and Constantinople were great rivals, and in 1202 the Venetians persuaded the soldiers of the Fourth Crusade to sack Constantinople instead of attacking the Turks, but after fifty years the Byzantines gained control once more. The Seljuk Turks were followed by the Ottoman Turks, and in 1453 came the final assault, and the last emperor died fighting on the walls. 1123 years after the foundation of Constantinople, the Byzantine Empire came to an end, but the city itself went on to become the capital of a great Turkish Empire. Constantinople is now the modern city of Istanbul.

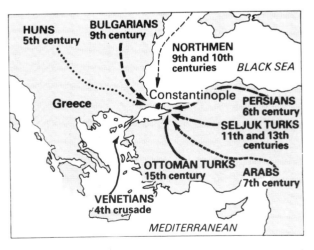

Exercises and things to do

1 Write out, filling in the blanks. One – stands for each missing letter.

In the Middle Ages most cities centred round the —————— or —————————, and the —————— place. Some of the earliest cities were in —————. The chief ones were —————, —————, ——————, and ————————. By the thirteenth century the Flemish cities of —————, ——————, and ——————— were rich from trading in —————. Cities in lands near the Baltic Sea formed the ————————— League. They were governed by the —————————.

Constantinople had been a great city from ————— times. It was the capital of the Eastern or ————————— Empire, and the centre of the Eastern —————————Church.

2 The heads and tails of these statements have been mixed. Write them out correctly.

(a) Cities of the Baltic	(1) were controlled by lords of the manor.
(b) Hanseatic town councils	(2) were absorbed by the rulers of the various Italian states.
(c) The English towns	(3) formed the Hanseatic League.
(d) Ghent	(4) was the last of the Italian city states.
(e) Venice	(5) was a wool manufacturing city.
(f) Italian towns	(6) excluded nobles from power.

3 *Statements of fact*. Write out the four statements in each group in what you think is their order of importance or interest. Say in each group why you have decided to put one particular statement first.

(a) Cities grew up
    (1) gradually during the Middle Ages.
    (2) round the castle, church and market.
    (3) as a result of trade and the setting up of a market.
    (4) where a church could form a centre of religious and other activities, and a market helped trade.

(b) The cities of the Middle Ages
    (1) were usually fairly small.
    (2) had narrow winding streets.
    (3) were centres of much life and activity.
    (4) had their own armies and protective walls.

(c) Constantinople
    (1) was named after Constantine, the Roman Emperor.
    (2) was almost surrounded by non-Christian peoples.
    (3) was a great centre of trade routes.
    (4) overcame attacks by non-Christian Persians, Turks and Northmen.

4 *The right order*. Write these down in the order in which they happened.

(a) Arabs attacked Constantinople by sea.
(b) Flemish merchants became rich and prosperous.
(c) Northmen attacked Constantinople.
(d) Ottoman Turks captured Constantinople.
(e) Venice became a great trading centre.

5 *The main idea*. Write down the one sentence which tells what you think is the main idea of this topic.

(a) The free cities of the Middle Ages were great centres of trade, religion and civilization.
(b) Towns grew into cities which governed themselves.
(c) The free cities often had public baths, hospitals and alms houses.
(d) The free cities often had their own armies and sometimes fought one another, or countries which attacked them.

6 Look at the picture of Carcassonne. Try to draw a plan of the town (as if you were looking at it from above) and show the walls, the castle, the church and some houses.

7 Which do you think would be (a) the easiest and (b) the most difficult parts of Carcassonne to attack during the Middle Ages?

8 Look in the library for books on the following English towns: York, Chester, Norwich and Lincoln. Draw one picture of each of these towns showing how they have streets like those in Rouen.

You can still see the houses of the Middle Ages in parts of Rouen in France.

10 New ideas and new sea-ways

After Rome

After the fall of the Roman Empire, the people of Europe discarded much of the civilized style of life which had come with the Romans. Such science as the Romans had developed was put aside, and many of the arts of good farming, gardening and fruit growing, and the manufacturing of all kinds of goods were abandoned. For centuries far fewer books were written, and also fewer people could read or write. These have been called the 'Dark Ages'.

They were long years of disorder, with raids by Vikings, Hungarians and Saracens. The nobles were sometimes little more than leaders of robber bands, often fighting one another, and plundering the village people. But slowly life became more ordered, since many ordinary people wanted to live in peace. This was a time of very slow change: the serfs expected to go on working just as their parents had done; craftworkers operated according to the rules of their guild, which did not alter from generation to generation.

New learning

Then, gradually, people began to work out new ideas, or rediscovered the old ones, and a new sort of civilization grew up in the Middle Ages. Fine cathedrals were built, schools and universities were started, though for a long time scarcely anyone studied science. People believed that everything was controlled by magic and miracles. Plague and natural disasters were thought to be God's punishments for sin, and little was done to find out the causes of diseases, or logical ways of combating them.

The Crusades brought the Europeans into contact with new ideas. The Moslems had doctors, gardeners, astronomers and other scientists far better than those of Europe. The crusaders often returned to their homes bringing with them booty captured from the Moslems. They told of the new foods they had eaten, the fine cities of the East and the luxuries from the distant countries of which they had heard.

New ideas at sea

Europeans became interested in new ideas from other countries and began to invent and discover new methods of their own. Sea captains began to work out better methods of shipbuilding and navigation. Until then seamen had depended upon the sun and stars to guide them, and a long spell of cloudy weather could make it impossible for a ship's captain to know in what direction he was sailing. The compass, which first came into use in Europe about AD 1300, enabled seamen to steer their way in any weather. It was probably invented in the highly civilized empire of China.

For a time people still felt no particular desire to make long voyages, or to find out about the unknown parts of the world. Their type of rudder and rigging made it impossible to sail into the wind, so even if a ship's captain had a compass, he might not be able to sail on the course he wanted to follow.

By the early fifteenth century a new rudder had been developed from the old steering oar, and three-masted ships were in general use. A new type of rigging made it possible to sail very close to the wind, so that a ship could sail more directly towards its destination. See box on page 56.

As people travelled further afield, they came back with stories of the strange things they had seen in foreign lands. This picture shows some of the people they described. Perhaps they made their stories up, or perhaps they really did see some of these weird monsters.

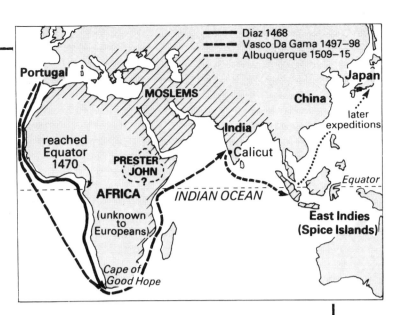

The way to India

At that time Europeans were unwelcome in the whole of North Africa, and the rest of that great continent was completely unknown. Europeans were also barred from almost the whole of Asia by the Moslems, while eastern Europe was increasingly being added to the Moslem territories. Nothing was known of the north-east. To the west the Atlantic was a barrier to travel. How far it stretched, and what lay beyond it was unknown, but Europeans were beginning to be interested in exploration, partly to spread the Christian religion, and partly to find gold and new sources of trade.

Prince Henry the Navigator

The Portuguese took the lead. They had gradually driven the Moslems out of their country, and by the beginning of the fifteenth century the whole of Portugal was free, and they were looking for ways of carrying the struggle against the Moslems into North Africa. Their Prince Henry the Navigator had heard of a mysterious Christian king called Prester John, who ruled a mighty kingdom somewhere in the east, perhaps in east Africa. If he could link up with Prester John, they might surround the Moslems, and bring Christianity to all Africa; then, having sailed round Africa, he might find a direct route to India and the Spice Islands. If Portuguese ships could sail all the way to India, they would be able to buy the precious goods which were so expensive in Europe, and sell them more cheaply while still making big profits.

Prince Henry studied maps, engaged skilful shipbuilders and navigators, and sent out sea captains to sail southwards along the west African coast.

India at last

Each expedition reached a little further. They passed the desert shores and reached the land of the rivers, forests and dark-skinned people. They traded for gold, took some slaves and returned home. The next ship reached a bit further, but progress was slow. Prince Henry died, his dream unfulfilled, but the voyages continued. In 1470 the Equator was reached. In 1486 Bartholomew Diaz passed round the south of Africa, round the Cape of Good Hope, into the Indian Ocean, and in 1498 Vasco da Gama reached Calicut in India. He took on a cargo of pepper, cloves, ginger, incense, tea, coffee and sugar, and returned home, where the goods were sold for high prices. But the price of the voyage in lives had also been high: two-thirds of the seamen who had set out from Portugal had died of scurvy.

Fleets of ships followed the course of Vasco da Gama, and pressed on past India to the Spice Islands in 1511. These East Indies were the main source of spices, and a rich trade developed. By the middle of the sixteenth century China and Japan had been reached.

The new trade routes were a great blow to the prosperity of Venice, for the Portuguese took their cargoes of precious eastern goods to Antwerp and other ports in north-western Europe which had previously obtained them from Venice. The trade of the Hanseatic cities was also threatened.

Vasco da Gama

Exercises and things to do

cinnamon

1 Write out, filling in the blanks. One – stands for each missing letter.

During the early Middle Ages, a new kind of ———————— was growing up in western ——————. Schools and ———————— were started, and much was learned from the Moslem —————— and ————————; but for a long time most people thought that plagues and misfortunes were sent by ——— as ———————— for sin.

Great improvements in ship ————————, methods of sailing and ———————— vessels made it possible to make long ——————— of discovery, and the ———————— found the way to ————— round the south of ——————.

cloves

2 The heads and tails of these statements have been mixed. Write them out correctly.

(a) The crusaders   (1) sailed to India in 1497–8
(b) The compass   (2) replaced the old steering oar.
(c) Vasco da Gama   (3) was believed to be a Christian king somewhere in Africa.

coffee

(d) Prester John   (4) learned about new things and ideas from the Moslems.

(e) The rudder   (5) enabled sailors to direct their course.

ginger

incense

> The new trade routes meant that Europeans could use foods they had never tasted before. Soon they were using lots of spices in their cooking. Here is a fifteenth-century recipe for a fruit tart. How is it different from the way you would make a fruit tart?
>
> Take figs and boil them in wine and grind them small . . . Put them in a vessel and add thereto powder pepper, cannell (cinnamon), cloves, mace, powder ginger, great raisins, saffron and salt. Then make a fair, low coffin (pastry case) and put this stuff therein. Put thereto cut dates and fresh salmon in fair pieces or else fresh eels and boil them in a little wine. Cover the coffin with the same paste and put into the oven to bake.

3 *Statements of fact.* Write out the four statements in each group, in what you think is their order of importance or interest. Say in each group why you have decided to put one particular statement first.

(a) Changes in shipping and navigation
  (1) were mainly concerned with rigging and rudders.
  (2) enabled seamen to keep on course without depending upon the sun and stars.
  (3) increased control over direction, and made steering more accurate in any weather.
  (4) enabled long voyages of discovery to be made.

(b) The Portuguese began voyaging along the coast of Africa
  (1) under the influence of Prince Henry the Navigator.
  (2) because they wanted to persuade other peoples to become Christian.
  (3) to try to link up with Prester John in an attack upon the Moslems.
  (4) to find a sea route by which they could take the Moslems in the rear, and also trade directly with India.

(c) The sea route from Portugal to India
  (1) was opened in 1497–8 by Vasco da Gama in a voyage round south Africa.
  (2) resulted from the efforts of Prince Henry the Navigator.
  (3) was a very long way round south Africa and across the Indian Ocean.
  (4) was the result of voyages by Bartholomew Diaz and other sailors.

4 *The right order.* Write these down in the order in which they happened.

(a) The death of Prince Henry the Navigator.
(b) The Moslems conquered Spain and Portugal.
(c) Vasco da Gama reached India.
(d) Bartholomew Diaz rounded the Cape of Good Hope.

5 *The main idea.* Write down the one sentence which tells what you think is the main idea of this topic.

(a) The signs of civilization grew scarcer in the 'Dark Ages', but became stronger again in the Middle Ages, partly from the influence of the Moslems.
(b) Europeans became interested in explorations in the fifteenth century in order to spread Christianity and increase trade.
(c) Changes in seamanship enabled the Portuguese to discover a sea route to India.

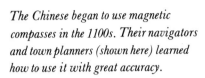
The Chinese began to use magnetic compasses in the 1100s. Their navigators and town planners (shown here) learned how to use it with great accuracy.

mace

6 Look in the library for a book with information on Prince Henry the Navigator. Write a short story about his life. You may wish to illustrate your story.

7 (a) Why were spices considered to be useful in the Middle Ages?
  (b) Make a list of the spices shown on this page.
  (c) List the ways in which you are able to add flavour to your food today.

8 (a) Find out how a compass works.
  (b) What else would you need to help you find your way about?
  (c) Who would need to use a compass?

9 Write out what you think part of the logbook of Vasco da Gama's ship may have described.

10 Write a conversation between Vasco da Gama and the Indian in charge at Calicut.

nutmeg

pepper

An early picture of a Portuguese merchant in India

saffron (crocus)

tea

11 The story of early India

India is like a huge island. To the south, south-west and south-east lies the ocean, and on the landward side are vast mountain ranges, cutting off the Indian plains from the rest of Asia. Although these mountains are a great barrier to ordinary travel, there are high passes, and many invaders have swooped down upon the people of the plain.

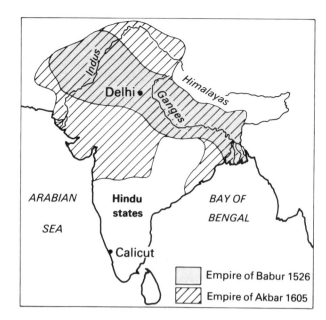

The Aryans
One of the oldest civilizations in the world existed nearly five thousand years ago in the valley of the Indus. This was ended about 1500 BC, probably by nomads from the north, people often known as Aryans. Most of the people of India at that time were dark-skinned Dravidians, who lived in villages and herded cattle. The Aryans were fair-skinned. Over many centuries they wandered through much of western Asia and Europe, taking with them their flocks and herds. They were better soldiers than the Dravidians, and had better weapons, using war chariots, bows and arrows and weapons of copper.

They gradually moved from the Indus valley eastwards, conquering the people of the Ganges valley. In some parts they drove them into the south of India, in others they mixed with them, or made them slaves to work in the fields, for by that time they were living a settled life. They probably learned city-building from the people of the Ganges valley, who were already town-dwellers.

The Aryans worshipped various gods, and a new religion grew up, with ideas from both races. This was known as Hinduism, which means 'Indian religion'. It is now the religion of several hundred million people. They worship many gods, and have thousands of images of them in their temples.

The Huns
In the fifth century AD the Huns of central Asia tried to force their way into northern India, but the Gupta kings who had gained power in AD 320 defeated them and they turned westwards towards Europe. More Huns and other Mongol tribes followed, and the north-west fell under their rule. They settled with Hindu wives, and in time merged with the Hindus.

The Moslems
In the eighth century the Moslems moved against India. They claimed that God had handed over India to them, the 'true believers', to plunder. They destroyed temples and smashed the idols. They slaughtered the 'idolaters', men, women and children. 'The whole country of India is full of gold and jewels,' wrote one of them, 'the whole aspect of the country is pleasant and delightful. Now since the inhabitants are chiefly infidels and idolaters, by order of God and his Prophet, it is right of us to conquer them.' Gradually the Moslems extended their power over the greater part of India.

The Mongols
Early in the thirteenth century the Mongol hordes led by Genghis Khan invaded the north and spread terror far and wide. They turned back at Peshawar, and swept out of India to the west.

Various kings ruled in Delhi, having great power over the people. Ibn Battuta, a great Arab traveller from Tangier, visited the city in 1342 and wrote of the king, 'Muhammed above all men delights most in giving presents and shedding blood. At his door is seen always some pauper on the way to wealth, or some corpse that has been executed. The rites of religion are observed at his court; he is most strict about prayer and the punishment of those who neglect it.'

Timur the Lame
From 1351 to 1388 there was peace in India. Great canals for irrigation schemes were dug, and many beautiful gardens laid out. But then Timur the Lame of the Mongols invaded India. In 1398 he crossed the Indus with 90000 cavalry, and advanced upon Delhi. An Indian army with 120 gigantic war elephants plated with armour

A picture of Akbar's tomb near Agra. Agra was his capital city and from there Akbar controlled his vast empire.

opposed him. Timur protected his front with tethered buffaloes, while his horsemen attacked the Indians in the rear. The elephants stampeded and trampled down their own people, and Timur swept into Delhi. The city was sacked and its people slaughtered. In the spring Timur withdrew from India, leaving a terrible trail of desolation. Mongolian khans were left to rule the country.

The Mogul Empire

At the end of the fifteenth century a new force entered the history of India: the Europeans arrived. In 1498 some little Portuguese ships visited Calicut to trade. Little notice was taken of them, as another great Mongol Empire had been established. It was known as the Mogal or Mughal Empire. Its founder was Babur, who was said to be so strong that he could run along the battlements, leaping over the gaps, with a man under each arm. He was also fond of poetry, and the

beauty of nature. He was probably the first leader to use gunpowder on a big scale. His grandson Akbar extended the Mogal Empire over almost the whole of India, creating an empire greater in extent than all the countries of western Europe put together.

Scholars and merchants from many countries came to Akbar's court. Although Akbar was a Moslem, he did not reserve all the important positions in the government for Moslems, but gave Hindus and people of all races and religions an opportunity to serve the country. He wanted his empire to be an Indian one, not just a Mongol or a Moslem one.

It was during his reign that the first Englishmen came to India, with messages from Queen Elizabeth I. A new and unexpected chapter in India's history was beginning.

47

Exercises and things to do

1 Write out, filling in the blanks. One – stands for each missing letter.

One of the oldest civilizations in the world was in India, in the ————— valley. About ———— BC the fair-skinned ————— people moved across India and conquered the darker-skinned —————————— who lived in towns and villages. Both races worshipped many ————, and in some places they lived together, and the religion of ———————— grew up.

India was invaded in the fifth century by the ————, but the ————— kings drove them out. Then other —————— tribes conquered the north-west and settled there. In the eighth century the ———————— conquered much of the country. In the thirteenth century the ——————— led by ——————— ———— invaded the north, but then moved away —————————. Then came a time of peace, and —————— were dug, and ———————— made, but in AD 1398 the ——————— led by ————— invaded the country and sacked —————.

A great empire was set up, called the ————— Empire, and King ————— is considered to have been one of the world's best rulers.

2 The heads and tails of these definitions have been mixed. Write them out correctly.

(a) Indus	(1) ruler of the Mogal Empire
(b) Hinduism	(2) founder of the Mogal Empire
(c) Timur	(3) the river in whose valley the first Indian civilization grew up
(d) Akbar	(4) Mongol leader who sacked Delhi in 1398
(e) Babur	(5) the main religion of India

3 *Statements of fact.* Write out the statements in each group in what you think is their order of importance or interest. Say in each group why you have decided to put one particular statement first.

(a) India
   (1) has high mountains in the north.
   (2) has ocean to the south-east and south-west.
   (3) is part of Asia.
   (4) is surrounded by mountains and sea.

(b) The Mongols who invaded India
   (1) under Genghis Khan spread terror in the north, but then left the country.
   (2) under Timur the Lame did terrible damage.
   (3) did not conquer the whole country.

(c) The Mogal Empire
   (1) was founded by Babur.
   (2) was in existence when the first Europeans visited India.
   (3) was enlarged by Akbar who welcomed scholars of many races at his court.

4 *The right order.* Write these down in the order in which they happened.

(a) Akbar ruled India.
(b) The Moslems conquered much of northern India.
(c) The first Englishmen visited India.
(d) Genghis Khan invaded India.
(e) Portuguese traders first went to India.

5 *The main idea.* Write down the one sentence which tells what you think is the main idea of this topic.

(a) India is like an island.
(b) India had a long history of civilization and invasion.
(c) Akbar was a very good ruler who brought different races and religions together.
(d) India was invaded by Aryans, Huns, Greeks, Moslems and Mongols.

6 On an outline map of India mark in

(a) Calcutta	Also mark in
(b) Delhi	
(c) River Ganges	(g) The Himalayas
(d) Bombay	(h) The Arabian Sea
(e) Madras	(i) The Bay of Bengal
(f) Agra	(j) The Indian Ocean

7 Here are some names: Calicut, Delhi, Gupta, Mogal, Mongol, Moslem. Which of them was

(a) the name of a Hindu family of kings
(b) a believer in the Mohammedan religion
(c) a nomad of central Asia
(d) the capital city of India at one time
(e) the name of the last empire in India before the English took part in ruling India
(f) an Indian port visited by the Portuguese in 1498.

The Mogul Emperor Akbar (1542–1605) tried to unite all the peoples of India. Here he and his friends are seen hunting with trained cheetahs. Servants follow to collect the prey.

8 Draw a map of India to show it as an 'island', and show the routes by which various invaders reached this 'island'. Name the seas and mountains they would have crossed to reach it.

9 What was going on in India when the following events were occurring in other parts of the world?

(a) The Stone Age in England was ending about 1800 BC.
(b) The barbarians were beginning to attack the Roman Empire about AD 300.
(c) King John sealed the Magna Carta in 1215.
(d) The Black Death was raging in England.

10 Copy the map showing Akbar's Empire.

12 The story of early Africa

An early African civilization

Africa was the home of one of the earliest and greatest civilizations in the world. Five thousand years ago, when the people of Britain were still living in the Stone Age, Egyptians were building fine cities and temples, making beautiful objects of metal and writing books. This Egyptian civilization lasted far longer than that of ancient Greece and Rome. After three thousand years as a leading power, she became an important part of the Roman Empire. The greatest centre of Greek science in the Greek and Roman world was the Egyptian city of Alexandria.

The Roman Empire fell, and Europe moved into the less eventful time of the 'Dark Ages', but in AD 639 Egypt, and soon afterwards all of north Africa, became part of the great Arab Moslem civilization and adopted the Arab religion, language and culture. Universities were built and important advances made in science.

The land of the Negroes

To the south of the Moslems lay the vast Sahara Desert, and beyond that the land which belonged to the Negroes. This was a wide belt of country stretching from the Atlantic to the Red Sea, cut off in the south by tropical forest and surf-ridden shores where fever lurked, and no beast of burden could live because of the tsetse fly. Very gradually the taller Negroes, including the Bantu and other dark-skinned peoples, moved southwards, driving the smaller Pygmies, Hottentots and Bushmen into the dense forests or the inhospitable desert. Meanwhile Arabs were also moving southwards along the coastal lands of east Africa, taking them under their control.

Negro kingdoms

In the eleventh century other Arabs moved up the Nile valley, and then turned westwards, south of the Sahara Desert. They gained power over the Negro kings. Towns were built, and trade was carried on across the Sahara. Gold and slaves were sent northwards, while salt came southwards from the desert. One of the Negro kingdoms somewhere near the upper River Niger was called Ghana (not to be confused with the modern country of Ghana). It was described in 1066 by Al-Bakri, an Arab scholar from Cordoba in Spain: 'Ghana con-

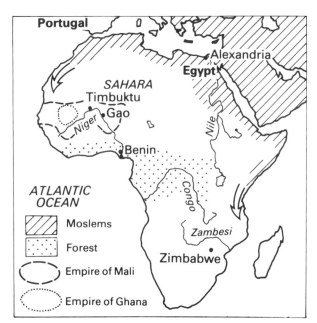

sists of two towns situated in a plain. The one inhabited by Muslims is very big and includes twelve mosques. The town the king lives in is 10 kilometres away. The territory between the two towns is covered with dwellings. The houses are built of stone and wood.'

Dumb barter

Trade was carried on between Ghana merchants and the gold miners by 'dumb barter'. The merchants set out their goods on the bank of the river and retired out of sight. The miners then approached and put down the amount of gold dust they thought reasonable, and retired. The merchants returned, and if satisfied, took the gold and departed, and the miners came and collected the goods. If the merchants thought the gold insufficient, they would not take it, and retired. The miners would then add more gold, until agreement was reached.

The Negroes of Ghana adopted the Moslem religion, and their kingdom grew in size and power, until it became a considerable empire, reaching almost 1600 kilometres from the Atlantic coast to the River Niger and far along its course. The Ghana Empire flourished for centuries, but by 1350 it had broken up, and the Mali Empire, even larger, took its place.

The Mali Empire

Ibn Battuta, the Arab traveller, visited Mali in

1353. He wrote that the Sultan of Mali was preceded by his musicians, who carried gold and silver guitars, and behind him came three hundred slaves. 'The Negroes,' wrote Battuta, 'are seldom unjust, and have a greater abhorrence of injustice than any other people. There is complete security in their country. Neither traveller nor inhabitant in it has anything to fear from robbers or men of violence.' Such a thing could not have been said of England at that time.

The Mali Empire weakened in the late fourteenth century, and the Songhai Empire of Gao spread until it stretched even more widely than Mali had done. Timbuktu became a great city with a famous university. Leo Africanus, a Moslem traveller from Granada in Spain, wrote of it, 'There are numerous judges, doctors and clerics in Timbuktu, all receiving good salaries from the king. There is a big demand for books; more profit is made from the book trade than from any other line of business.'

Zimbabwe

Meanwhile in east Africa the Arabs had built up a very prosperous trade in gold, slaves and ivory. Between the eleventh and the fourteenth centuries an African kingdom had grown up some way inland round Zimbabwe, from which the modern country of Zimbabwe takes its name. There in a valley was a vast enclosure with massive stone walls. Inside were other stone buildings and a solid conical tower. There is no other quite like it anywhere in the world. Above were stone hill forts. Little is known about the people who built them.

The coming of the Europeans

Whether the African kingdoms would have developed further and built a great African civilization we do not know, for the coming of Europeans brought changes. The Africa of the Middle Ages was hostile to Europeans: in the north were the Moslems, who fought the Europeans in the Crusades, and raided European shipping in the Mediterranean. Further south nature was hostile, exposing the European explorers first to the arid sands of the desert, then to the dismal mangrove swamps and deadly diseases of the unhealthy tropical lands. The Portuguese, however, were not deterred, and trading posts were set up on the coast. Africans brought gold, slaves, ivory, pepper and other things to them. Gradually the trade and prosperity of the Negro kingdoms between the desert and the forest were forced out of existence.

An African ivory casket which was probably used as a salt store. The figures represent Portuguese dignitaries.

Exercises and things to do

1 Write out, filling in the blanks. One – stands for each missing letter.

One of the world's first great civilizations grew up in the African country of – – – – –. The Egyptian city of – – – – – – – – – became an important centre of – – – – – and – – – – – science. After the fall of the Roman Empire, North – – – – – – became part of the – – – – civilization, and the – – – – – – religion and science were studied at the – – – – – – – – – of Cairo in Egypt.

Further south in Africa, the dark-skinned – – – – – – – gradually conquered the – – – – – – –, – – – – – – – and – – – – – – – – – –. The Arabs were also moving southwards, up the valley of the – – – – and along the – – – – coast, where they traded in – – – – – –, – – – –, and – – – – –.

2 The heads and tails of these statements have been mixed. Write them out correctly.

(a) The first part of Africa to be civilized	(1) was Ghana.
(b) Ibn Battuta	(2) traded by 'dumb barter'.
(c) The first Negro empire south of the Sahara	(3) was Egypt.
(d) Ghana merchants and the gold miners	(4) described the empire of Mali.
(e) Timbuktu	(5) had great stone buildings, but we know little about their builders.
(f) Zimbabwe	(6) was a university city.

A bronze head found at Ife in Nigeria. Bronze sculptures were made between AD 1000 and the 1400s.

3 *Statements of fact.* Write out the four statements in each group in what you think is their order of importance or interest. Say in each group why you have decided to put one particular statement first.

(a) Egypt
  (1) was civilized long before Britain.
  (2) had a longer history of civilization than any country in Europe.
  (3) was part of Roman civilization.
  (4) was an important part of Arab and Moslem civilization.

(b) In Africa south of the Sahara
  (1) the people were mainly Negroes.
  (2) Arabs gained power over Negro kings.
  (3) Negro kingdoms, influenced by Arabs, were built up in the Middle Ages.
  (4) Timbuktu became an important university city.

(c) The Negroes south of the Sahara
  (1) adopted Arab religion and many Arab customs.
  (2) traded by 'dumb barter'.
  (3) were described by Ibn Battuta as being very just.
  (4) set up a Moslem civilization in which justice was done and books were highly prized.

4 *The right order.* Write these down in the order in which they happened.

(a) Timbuktu became a great city of Gao.
(b) Egypt became a home of civilization.
(c) Africans sold gold and slaves to the European traders on the west African coast.
(d) Ghana became a Negro empire.
(e) The Arabs conquered Egypt.

5 *The main idea.* Write down the one sentence which tells what you think is the main idea of this topic.

(a) The Negroes lived between the desert and the tropical forest.
(b) The Mali Empire stretched for nearly 1600 kilometres.
(c) Egyptians, Negroes and Arabs had all achieved quite a high degree of civilization in Africa long before the Europeans went there.
(d) The Africans at first exchanged goods by dumb barter, but later developed normal trade.

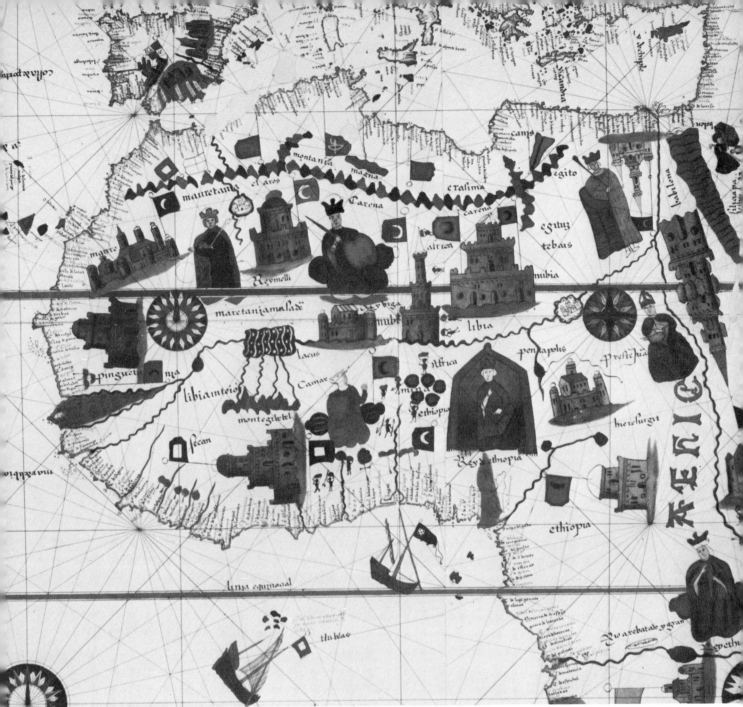

6 What was happening in Africa when the following things were happening in Europe?

(a) The British people were living as hunters and gatherers in the Stone Age before there was much farming.
(b) The conquest of Britain by the Saxons was coming to an end.
(c) The Battle of Hastings.
(d) Europe was recovering from the Black Death.
(e) England was settling down after the Peasants' Revolt.

7 Draw a map of Africa north of the Equator, and colour it as follows: black for the land of the Negroes, green for the tropical forest, yellow for the desert, white for the land inhabited mainly by Arabs, and blue for the sea.

This map of part of Africa was drawn by European discoverers in 1500. Compare it with the modern map on page 50 to see how accurate their outline was.

8 Here are some names: Arabs, Bantu, Hottentots, Mali, Moslems, Sahara, Tsetse. Which of them means

(a) a Negro empire south of the Sahara
(b) dark-skinned African people
(c) a fly which causes disease
(d) a desert
(e) fair-skinned people in north Africa
(f) believers in the Mohammedan religion
(g) African people driven south by the Negroes.

9 Look at the early map of Africa above. Why do you think so many places at the coast are labelled and so few inland?

53

13 The way to America

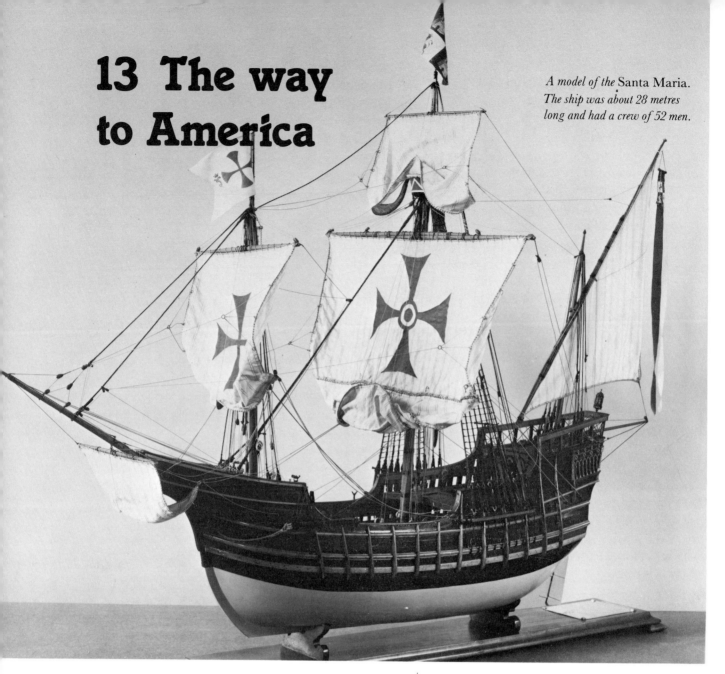

A model of the Santa Maria. The ship was about 28 metres long and had a crew of 52 men.

The ancient Greeks discovered a great deal about the earth. A scientist called Eratosthenes believed that it was a sphere, and about 200 BC he succeeded in measuring it fairly accurately. About AD 150 Ptolemy drew maps of the world and calculated its size, but the figure he arrived at was a good deal too small.

Lost knowledge

During the so-called Dark Ages this knowledge was lost, and people again believed that the earth was flat. Sailors were afraid to sail into unknown seas as they feared that they might fall over the edge of the world. But during the Middle Ages some of the old Greek knowledge was brought to the West, largely by Moslem scholars, and by the fifteenth century most educated Europeans believed that the earth was round. They were anxious to open up direct trade with the Far East, the Spice Islands, India, Cathay (China) and

Japan. Once it was believed that the earth was round it became clear that it must be possible to reach the Far East by sailing westwards.

Christopher Columbus

Christopher Columbus, a Genoese seaman, believed this, and he believed that he was the person to prove it. He studied the ideas of Ptolemy, and thought that the world was about 29 000 kilometres in circumference. The maps of the time made Asia appear to be larger than it really is, so it stretched much further eastwards. Columbus therefore thought that a voyage of five or six thousand kilometres across the Atlantic would bring him to the shores of China and Japan.

Queen Isabella of Spain agreed to fit out a small expedition for Columbus. He had three ships, the *Santa Maria*, of one hundred tons, and the *Pinta* and *Nina*, about half that size. The crews totalled about 120 men, some of them criminals who were

54

willing to risk the voyage rather than stay in prison.

Into the unknown

Columbus sailed from Spain on 3 August 1492, called at the Canary Isles, and then set course for the unknown. After thirty-three days they reached a small island. Columbus was rowed ashore. He unfurled the flag of Spain, set up a large cross, and knelt before it, thanking God for a successful voyage. Then he sailed on and discovered other islands, including Cuba and Haiti. They were, he said, 'very beautiful, with many kinds of birds and fruits. The natives were timid, and without iron or steel weapons.' But there were no fine cities, no wealth of gold, none of the spices which were almost worth their weight in gold.

Nevertheless, Columbus was sure that he had reached his goal. The islands, he decided, must be those off the coast of India, and he called them the Indies. They are still called the West Indies, even though they are on the opposite side of the world from the real Indies. He had sailed a little over 6000 kilometres. It was nearly another 20000 to the real Indies.

At Haiti the *Santa Maria* struck a reef, and Columbus transferred to the *Nina*. There was not room for all, so he built a fort, and left a colony of Spaniards there to await his return.

A second voyage

Columbus arrived home in triumph, and prepared for another voyage. There were plenty of volunteers this time, and he had three large ships and fourteen smaller ones, and 1500 men. He found that the men he had left on Haiti had been killed, so he hopefully founded another settlement. He sailed for hundreds of kilometres along the south coast of Cuba, and decided that it must be part of the mainland of Asia. His return this time was far from triumphant. He brought no rich spoils, and his men were weak and ill.

The end of twenty years of toil

Still believing he had discovered the way to the riches of the East, he made a third journey. He sailed along part of the mainland of South America, but did not realize this. In 1503 he made yet another voyage, and sailed along the Central American coast. He thought, from what the natives told him, that he was somewhere near the River Ganges. The weather was bad, the food was scant and rotten, and he himself was ill. When he got back to Spain, Queen Isabella, who had first trusted him, was dead, and he received no honours or reward for all his efforts. He died in 1506, a poor and disappointed man.

Amerigo's land

Other seamen followed Columbus, and in 1499 Amerigo Vespucci sailed along the coast of South America. He wrote a book about the new lands, and people spoke of Amerigo's land, and so gave it the name of America.

John Cabot

Meanwhile another Italian, John Cabot, living in Bristol, had the same idea as Columbus. He persuaded Henry VII that he could bring the wealth of Cipango (Japan) to England by sailing westwards. In 1497 he sailed in a tiny boat with a crew of eighteen. He discovered Newfoundland and returned, claiming that he had 'won a part of Asia without a stroke of the sword'.

Balboa

After Columbus, many Spaniards settled on the islands and the mainland of Central America. Vasco Nunez de Balboa became the leader of a group in Darien, where they heard from a chief that there was a great sea beyond the mountains, and that beyond that lay a land rich in gold. They set out and climbed the mountains. Then, leaving the others, Balboa went forward, and was the first Spaniard to see the Pacific Ocean. He knelt down with tears in his eyes, and thanked God for having allowed him to see something which none of his countrymen had ever seen. He called his men down, then, drawing his sword, he waded into the sea, and claimed it all for the King of Spain. He was made governor of Panama, and was soon building and launching ships on the Pacific, the first Spaniard to do so. Then the governor of Darien, who was jealous of him, arrested him and executed him for treason.

Exercises and things to do

Developments in ship-building

1 The use of 2–3 masts with a combination of square and triangular sails (borrowed from the Arabs, see page 6) made it possible for the ship to sail against the wind by tacking (zig-zagging).

wind

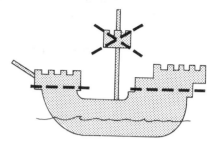

2 Improved design lowered the profile of the decks to give less wind resistance.

6 The hull was made better and stronger with a slimmer more streamlined shape.

5 The keel was invented to prevent the ship from being blown off course sideways when the wind was side on.

3 The rudder took the place of the old steering oar.

When the ship heeled over or the sea was rough, the steering oar lost its effectiveness.

wind

wind

Steering oar too deep to be effective – could snap under strain.

Steering oar almost out of contact with water – ship out of control.

4 Early ships had to carry a large crew of rowers to move the ship when the wind was against them.

wind

This was not good on long voyages when the rowers took up valuable cargo space, besides needing much food and drink. With better sail design (see 1) the rowers were not needed thus giving more cargo space.

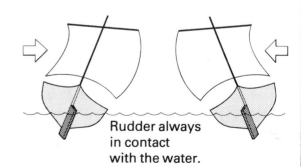

Rudder always in contact with the water.

The invention of the rudder meant that the ship could be steered no matter how much the ship heeled over or how rough the sea was.

1 Write out the following, filling in the blanks. One – stands for each missing letter.

In the early Middle Ages most of the people of Europe thought that the earth was ––––, but by the fifteenth century, the discovery by the ancient –––––– about the shape of the earth had been rediscovered, and most educated people believed it was –––––. This meant that if you wanted to reach the Far ––––, you could get there by going either –––––––– or ––––––––.

Christopher –––––––– was sure that he could do this by sailing ––––––––– across the –––––––– Ocean. In AD ––––, with the help of the Queen of –––––, he set out. He thought he would have to sail about 6000 kilometres to reach ––––– and the ––––– –––––––. To his great joy he did reach some islands at about that distance, but they were ––– the islands he was looking for, but part of a great new ––––––––. Although he did not know it, he had discovered ––––––––.

2 The heads and tails of these statements have been mixed. Write them out correctly.

(a) Ptolemy	(1) was the first European to see the Pacific.
(b) Isabella	(2) was the name of Columbus's ship.
(c) John Cabot	(3) discovered Haiti.
(d) Columbus	(4) discovered Newfoundland.
(e) Santa Maria	(5) was Queen of Spain.
(f) Balboa	(6) was a Greek who calculated the size of the earth.

3 *Statements of fact.* Write out the four statements in each group in what you think is their order of importance or interest. Say in each group why you have decided to put one particular statement first.

(a) The geographical knowledge of the ancient Greeks
  (1) was greater than that of the Europeans of the Dark Ages.
  (2) enabled them to map much of the world and to measure its size.
  (3) was forgotten during the Dark Ages.
  (4) was rediscovered in the Middle Ages, and led to great advances in astronomy and exploration.

(b) The fact that the earth is round
  (1) meant that the Far East could be reached by sailing westwards.
  (2) was discovered by Eratosthenes.
  (3) was recognized by most educated men in Europe by 1450.
  (4) led to a new interest in voyages of discovery.

(c) In the fifteenth century Europeans
  (1) wanted to find a sea route to the east by sailing westwards.
  (2) were looking for a way to get goods from the East more cheaply.
  (3) hoped to obtain cheaper spices and luxuries by new sea routes to the East.
  (4) sent ships both east and west to find sea routes to the Indies.

(d) Christopher Columbus
  (1) believed that he was the man to prove that the East could be reached across the Atlantic.
  (2) sailed westwards from Spain and reached the West Indies.
  (3) was a Genoese seaman who studied the ideas of Ptolemy.
  (4) was helped by Queen Isabella of Spain.

4 *The right order.* Write these down in the order in which they happened.
(a) Cabot discovered Newfoundland.
(b) Eratosthenes measured the earth.
(c) Columbus discovered the West Indies.
(d) Ptolemy calculated the size of the earth.

5 *The main idea.* Write down the one sentence which tells what you think is the main idea of this topic.

(a) Columbus opened up the Atlantic and America to exploration.
(b) Rediscovery of ancient Greek knowledge led to the discovery of America in the fifteenth century.
(c) Early explorers of the Atlantic did not realize the true size of the earth.
(d) Explorers seeking a good new route to the Far East found America instead.

6 You are a young sailor on your first voyage in a new ship like the one in this drawing. You are very excited about all the new developments it has. Write a letter to your father, who is very interested in ships, to tell him what is different about the way it looks and the way it sails.

14 From exploration to conquest: the Spaniards in America

Rumours of a rich native kingdom on the mainland of Mexico reached the Spaniards in the West Indies. In 1519 Hernando Cortes gathered a small group in Cuba and set out to take it from its inhabitants in the name of his religion. 'Brothers,' he said, 'follow the Cross in faith, for under its guidance we shall conquer. I promise you glory and riches but these can only be won by incessant toil. You are few, but strong in resolution. Be sure that God will never desert the Spaniard in his contest with the infidel.'

Cortes had about six hundred men, sixteen horses and fourteen small cannon. Some of the soldiers were alarmed at the idea of marching inland. Cortes ordered all the ships except one to be burned. 'If any are afraid,' he said, 'there is one ship left; let them go, and tell how they deserted their commander and their comrades. For my part, I go forward.' All his men shouted, 'To Mexico, to Mexico!' and they set out on the three hundred kilometre march.

Peru

Meanwhile the Spaniards in Panama heard rumours of a rich empire in Peru to the south. Francisco Pizarro gathered a band of men and set out to find it. On the way food was scarce, some men were killed, and others wanted to give up. Pizarro drew his sword and traced a line in the sand. 'Friends,' he said, pointing to the south, 'on that side are toil, hunger and death; on this side ease and pleasure; on that side the riches of Peru, on this side poverty in Panama. Each man choose as a brave Spaniard should. For my part, I go south.'

With an even smaller force than Cortes had in Mexico, Pizarro conquered the huge, rich empire of Peru, which extended for three thousand kilometres through the valleys of the Andes. Then he

Mexico City

Montezuma, the Emperor of Mexico, received the Spaniards kindly, and led them into the great city of Mexico, with its sixty thousand houses of stone and brick, its grand palaces and the temples used for human sacrifice. They were given one of the royal palaces to live in. Then, surrounded by tens of thousands of hospitable Aztec warriors, the small invading band of Spaniards ordered the emperor and all the people to give up their religion and adopt the European faith of Christianity. They seized Montezuma, and held him prisoner in the middle of his own capital city. Fighting broke out, and in a desperate retreat many of the Spaniards were killed or captured and sacrificed to the gods. Cortes wept, but he was not beaten. With a few hundred more soldiers who arrived from Cuba, he advanced against the city, and destroyed it building by building until the Aztecs gave in, and Mexico was forced to become a Spanish colony.

sent out exploring parties to find El Dorado, the fabled Land of Gold. One band crossed the mountains and descended into the densely forested valley of the Amazon. Their food was exhausted, but rather than return, they decided to sail down the river, further into the unknown. 'Having eaten our shoes and saddles boiled with a few wild herbs,' said Orellana, 'we set out to reach the kingdom of gold.'

Having eaten their horses, they used the horseshoes to make nails and built a river boat. They tore up their shirts to calk the ship's seams. Food was so short that men died almost daily. The river grew so wide that they could not see the other bank. Some natives were friendly, others attacked them. They met tribes where the women led the fighting, so they called the river the Amazon, after the women warriors of ancient Greece. In 1541, two years after setting out, they reached the sea. Making rigging from vines, and using blankets for sails, they put to sea and reached the West Indies, but they still had not found El Dorado.

Machu Pichu, an Inca city discovered in 1912. Built in the Andes mountains it was one of the main cities in an empire stretching 2,500 miles from north to south.

At the centre of Aztec cities were flat topped pyramids with temples on top. They were built by thousands of men and dedicated to Aztec gods.

Exercises and things to do

1 Write out, filling in the blanks. One – stands for each missing letter.

In 1519 Hernando ––––––– set out from –––– to conquer the rich empire of –––––– for Spain. He was anxious to convert the people to ––––––––––– but what many of his men wanted was –––––––. The Emperor ––––––––– welcomed the Spaniards, but they were horrified at the ––––– sacrifices, and tried to make the ––––– people and their ruler give up their ––––––––, and become Christians. They seized Montezuma and held him –––––––––. Then the Aztecs attacked them, and they were forced to ––––––– from the city.

Cortes obtained a few more ––––––––– and made a new assault on the city, destroying it bit by bit until the ––––––– were forced to give in, and Mexico became a Spanish –––––––.

Soon after, another Spanish leader named ––––––––– –––––––– conquered the even larger and ––––––– empire of ––––. He then sent out groups of men to explore the land, and try to find –– –––––––, the Land of ––––, of which they had heard rumours.

2 The heads and tails of these statements have been mixed. Write them out correctly.

(a) El Dorado   (1) was the great river explored by Orellana.

(b) Francisco Pizarro   (2) conquered the Aztecs.

(c) Montezuma   (3) was the Spanish conqueror of Peru.

(d) Hernando Cortes   (4) was the Emperor of Mexico.

(e) Amazon   (5) was the name of the Land of Gold.

3 *Statements of fact.* Write out the four statements in each group in what you think is their order of importance or interest. Say in each group why you have decided to put one particular statement first.

(a) The people of Mexico
  (1) were conquered by Cortes.
  (2) were called Aztecs.
  (3) were ruled by Montezuma.
  (4) made human sacrifices.

The Aztecs and Incas were skilled craftspeople. This drawing is of a gold Inca toucan, set with turquoises.

(b) The Spaniards who explored the Amazon
  (1) were led by Orellana.
  (2) ate their horses, shoes and saddles.
  (3) overcame great difficulties in their 3000 kilometre voyage.
  (4) reached the sea in 1541.

(c) The Spanish explorers in America
  (1) were driven by a thirst for gold.
  (2) wanted to convert the people to Christianity.
  (3) opened up vast areas with very small armies.
  (4) founded a great Spanish Empire.

A sixteenth century drawing shows a female Aztec interpreter standing between Spaniards and Indians translating their words. Many people in South America now speak Spanish.

4 *The right order.* Write these down in the order in which they happened.

(a) Pizarro conquered Peru.
(b) Orellana reached the sea.
(c) Mexico became a Spanish colony.
(d) Montezuma was made a prisoner.
(e) Cortes landed in Mexico.

5 *The main idea.* Write down the one sentence which tells what you think is the main idea of this topic.

(a) Cortes, Pizarro, Orellana and other Spaniards explored and conquered much of America.
(b) The Spaniards sailed to America to find gold and to convert the people to Christianity.
(c) Mexico, Peru and the Amazon were all explored in the early sixteenth century.
(d) There were large, well-organized empires in America which were conquered by the Spaniards.

6 What actions of Cortes do you think show that he was interested in more than just gaining wealth?

7 Write part of what the log of Orellana's expedition may have described.

8 Peruvian women wore a one-piece dress reaching to the ankles, and bound at the waist by a wide ornamental sash. The upper edges were fastened over the shoulders by long pins. They wore a kind of cloak over the shoulders and fastened at the front with a large-headed pin. The hair was parted in the middle and hung down the back. Make a drawing of Peruvian women wearing this type of dress.

9 What facts mentioned here about the Aztecs suggest that they had a strong civilization of their own? But why could they not withstand a small band of invaders?

10 Using the pictures on this page, draw or describe what Aztec women wore.

11 Look at the drawing of Aztec children at work. Describe what is happening in each picture.

12 Imagine you are the boy or girl in the picture. Tell a visiting Spaniard who you are and what you do. Don't forget to mention your age and how many tortillas you are allowed.

This is a drawing from an Aztec manuscript, showing children being taught by their parents. The words are shown coming out of the parents' mouths. The black dots show how old the child is and the circles show how many tortillas (pancakes) he or she was allowed each day. The boy in the bottom picture is being punished: he is being held over a fire of burning red peppers to make his eyes sting.

13 Look at the picture of the interpreter standing between the Spaniards and Aztecs. Copy the picture but show cartoon bubbles coming from the mouths of the people. Inside the bubbles write what you think the people are saying to each other.

15 Printing and new ideas

The fifteenth century was an exciting time in Europe. The restricted world of the Middle Ages was opening out into the larger world of modern times. Any day a ship might come into port with the news of fresh lands and peoples discovered, of new seas crossed and new routes opened. There were also many other new ideas in circulation. Some of them were really very old ones, first thought of by the ancient Greeks, and long forgotten in the West, although there were still copies of the old books containing this knowledge in Constantinople.

Precious books old and new

The Moslem scholars had known this ancient knowledge for centuries, and had translated the Greek books into Arabic. Gradually in the fourteenth and early fifteenth centuries, as the Turks over-ran more and more of eastern Europe, scholars from Constantinople fled to the West, particularly to Italy, taking some of these precious books with them. A new interest in books arose, and spread to France, Germany, the Netherlands, Poland and England, and other parts of Europe. New books were written, and physics, astronomy, geography and other sciences were studied.

Books in the Middle Ages had to be copied by hand, so they were very scarce and expensive; but as more and more people wanted books, inventors began to think about quicker ways of reproducing them. For centuries a very simple kind of printing had been used in making seals, and in the fourteenth century a wood block was sometimes cut for each whole page of a book, so that ink could be spread on the block and copies could be printed; but this was a slow and costly process.

Moveable type

Then came the great advance: in the early fifteenth century, single letters were made of metal. These could be fitted together to make words, and held in place in wooden frames. A whole page of a book could be put together quite quickly in this way. When as many copies as were needed had been printed, the letters, or type, could be taken apart and used to make up other books. It was a simple idea, but nobody had been encouraged to think of it until the new interest in learning made books and reading much more popular.

This invention of printing with moveable type enabled new ideas to spread rapidly. Almost all

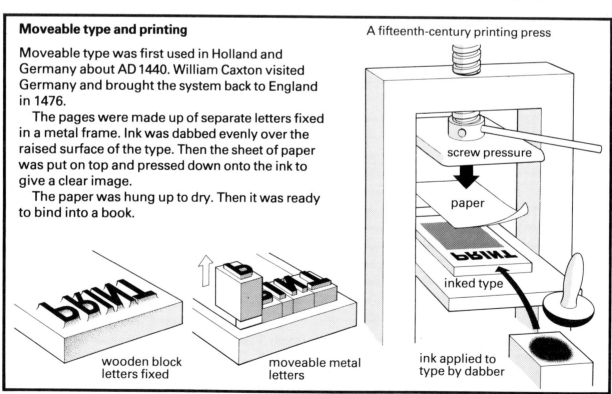

Moveable type and printing

Moveable type was first used in Holland and Germany about AD 1440. William Caxton visited Germany and brought the system back to England in 1476.

The pages were made up of separate letters fixed in a metal frame. Ink was dabbed evenly over the raised surface of the type. Then the sheet of paper was put on top and pressed down onto the ink to give a clear image.

The paper was hung up to dry. Then it was ready to bind into a book.

A fifteenth-century printing press

screw pressure

paper

inked type

wooden block letters fixed

moveable metal letters

ink applied to type by dabber

the books at that time were printed in Latin, because teaching at universities in most countries was in Latin, and so all scholars spoke Latin. An English scholar travelling through France, Holland, Germany, Poland, Italy and other countries in Europe would be able to discuss interesting questions with scholars and scientists everywhere without any language difficulty.

The moving earth

A famous Polish astronomer was Copernicus, 1473–1543. He discovered that the earth and the planets revolve round the sun. The Christian Church at that time taught that the earth was the centre of the universe, and that the sun, planets and stars were all small lights in the sky, moving round the earth. In those days people who said or wrote anything different from the teaching of the Church were likely to be put to death. Copernicus' book was banned, and he did not dare to publish it until he was an old man and at the point of death. Geordano Bruno, a fine scholar, was imprisoned for seven years because he believed that the ideas of Copernicus were true. He was told that he could go free if he admitted that the teaching of Copernicus was wrong. He refused, and the leaders of the Church had him burned to death in the year 1600. The new ideas upset many of the old Christian beliefs. Most people do not like having their beliefs questioned.

Another scientist was the Italian Galileo. He

Copernicus showed that the planets of the solar system, including the earth, keep moving around the sun.

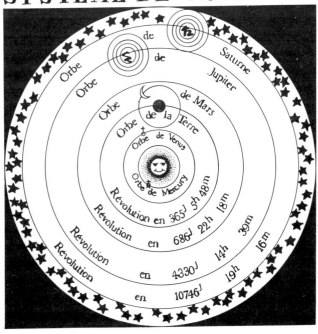

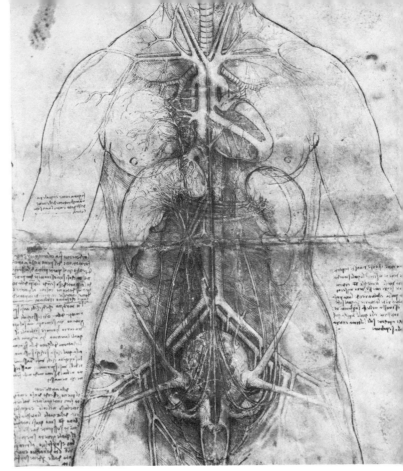

Leonardo da Vinci (1452–1519) was one of the world's greatest artists and designers. He was one of the first artists to study the workings of the body so that he could make his drawings as realistic as possible.

carried out many experiments, and improved the telescope which had been invented in Holland. This enabled him to prove that the ideas of Copernicus were right, and he wrote a book in their defence. The Pope ordered the book to be burned, and Galileo to be tried for publishing wicked ideas. The court threatened to burn him to death if he did not admit that he had been wrong. He decided to agree, and knelt down in the courtroom to swear that the earth did not move round the sun. It is said that as he got up, he said under his breath, 'It does move, all the same.' Galileo also invented a thermometer and a microscope.

Scholars in England

One English scholar was Sir Thomas More. He wrote a book called *Utopia*, in which he described an imaginary country where everything was arranged perfectly, and where all the things which he thought were done wrongly in the world of his day were put right.

One of the most famous scholars of the time was the Dutchman Erasmus. He did not think of himself as a Dutchman, but as a citizen of all Europe. He travelled from country to country, teaching and discussing. He taught for some years at Cambridge, and much enjoyed his stay in England. He was a friend of Sir Thomas More.

Exercises and things to do

1 Write out, filling in the blanks. One – stands for each missing letter.

In the Middle Ages books were written by ————, so they were scarce and very ————————. Early in the ———————— century a very important invention was made: single ——————— were made of —————. These were called ———— and they were fitted together in —————— frames to make —————, and so the whole page of a book could be printed quickly and as many copies as were wanted could easily be made. The first Englishman to set up a printing ————— was ——————— ———————.

New ideas of many kinds began to spread rapidly. Some of them upset the leaders of the Christian ——————, and when the astronomer —————————— said that the earth was not the —————— of the universe, but that it went ————— the ———, he dared not ——————— his book until he was an old man near to death.

2 The heads and tails of these statements have been mixed. Write them out correctly.

(a) Galileo	(1) was a famous Dutch scholar.
(b) William Caxton	(2) improved the telescope.
(c) Copernicus	(4) was put to death because of his beliefs.
(d) Geordano Bruno	(4) was the first English printer.
(e) Erasmus	(5) was a Polish astronomer.

3 *Statements of fact.* Write out the four statements in each group in what you think is their order of importance or interest. Say in each group why you have decided to put one particular statement first.

(a) Before printing was invented
  (1) books were scarce and expensive.
  (2) books were written by hand.
  (3) not many people in Europe could read.
  (4) few people read the expensive, hand-written books.

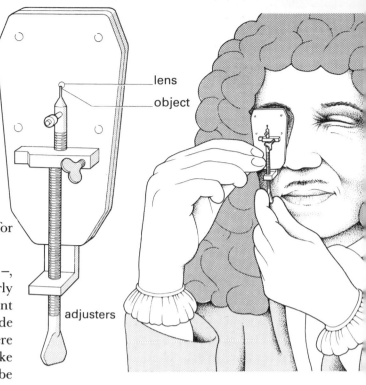

The microscope enlarges or magnifies objects placed underneath it. A Dutchman named Anton van Leeuwenhoek was the first man to discover germs. Germs are small living things which cannot be seen without a microscope. The microscope therefore helps doctors.

(b) The invention of printing
  (1) was brought to England by William Caxton.
  (2) occurred as soon as more people were able to read and became interested in books.
  (3) met a growing need for books in the fifteenth century.
  (4) sprang from the idea of making single metal letters.

(c) The new ideas about astronomy
  (1) brought Copernicus into conflict with the leaders of the Church who said that the earth did not go round the sun.
  (2) were due to Copernicus who lived in Poland.
  (3) were contrary to the ideas of the Church as to whether the earth was the centre of the universe.
  (4) were helped by Galileo's improvement of the telescope.

4 *The right order.* Write these down in the order in which they happened.

(a) the invention of single-letter moveable type.
(b) Caxton set up his printing press.
(c) Geordano Bruno was put to death.
(d) Copernicus published his book.
(e) Scholars began to flee from Constantinople when it came under Turkish attack.

5 *The main idea.* Write down the one sentence which tells what you think is the main idea of this topic.

(a) The fifteenth century was a time of new ideas which spread rapidly because of the invention of printing.
(b) The fifteenth century marked the ending of the Middle Ages and the beginning of modern times.
(c) Books became commoner and cheaper after the invention of printing.
(d) Printing was invented in Germany and brought to England.

6 Why do you think printing was invented in the fifteenth century and not before, say, in the tenth century?

7 Compare the drawing of the printing shop with the diagram on page 62. Find the dabber, the ink, the screw pressure and the type in the drawing. Why do you think the paper is hanging on a line?

8 Make up and act a play about the life of Galileo or Geordano Bruno.

9 If you were writing about a Utopia today, what things in the present world would you think were wrong, and how would your Utopian world be arranged so that they were put right?

10 Using this and other books write a short life story of either Copernicus, Galileo or Leonardo da Vinci.

11 Look for a book on lettering and copy out the alphabet in four different styles of writing.

12 Explain how the microscope works and say how it helps scientists and doctors.

13 Take a coin or another small object and draw a picture of it. Place the coin or object under a magnifying glass or microscope and draw what you can see.

An early engraving of a printing shop

Everyday life

A seventeenth-century etching by the famous artist Rembrandt showing a beggar family receiving money at the door of a rich man's house. Poverty was always a social problem in town and country areas. The Church had looked after the poor, but governments made no real efforts to deal with the problem. Parishes had to look after their own poor.

Another artist who painted the life of ordinary people was Peter Breughel. In this painting he portrays one of the gates of the rich trading city of Antwerp in Belgium. You can see fine buildings and people leaving and entering the city. Breughel also showed people skating and playing ice hockey. Can you see anyone being rescued?

66

A twelfth-century Chinese silk painting showing a spring festival on a river. There is much activity on the bridge and the artist has recorded many aspects of Chinese life. You can see stalls and tea shops, street traders, workers, people looking over the bridge, teachers and scholars, and people being carried in sedan chairs. In the background are buildings and also a house boat.

Look closely at the Breughel painting and the Chinese silk painting. In what ways are (a)–(f) similar or different in each painting?

(a) methods of travelling
(b) methods of carrying or transporting loads
(c) buildings
(d) bridges
(e) people's clothing
(f) weather

16 Changes in religion

The importance of religion

In the Middle Ages religion filled a much larger part in most people's lives than it does now. Many people went to church every day, and all went on Sundays. In all the churches the services were alike; there were no Baptist, Church of England, Congregational, Methodist or other churches in Britain. They were all Catholic, all looking up to the Pope as their head. The services were in Latin, the Bible was in Latin, the singing was in Latin, so, as the ordinary people did not understand Latin, they did not know very much about what Christ had really taught.

Dissatisfaction with the Church

People looked up to the Church, for it was the centre of the life of the town or village. It was the monks and clergy who also looked after the sick, the old and those in distress. They did not always do their work very well, and a few people became very dissatisfied with the selfishness and slackness of some of the churchmen. An important one of these was the Englishman John Wycliffe, 1320–84, who accused the Pope of being too fond of wealth and power. The Pope was obviously not pleased,

Some people disliked the power of the Catholic church. This German booklet called the pope 'Anti-Christ'. Even kings had to obey the pope.

but some leading people in England who did not like having to pay out large sums to Rome protected Wycliffe. When, however, he began translating the Bible into English, the leaders of the Church declared Wycliffe a heretic, and his books were burned, but his ideas were not forgotten. He had some followers, most of whom were poor people. They were called Lollards, and they wandered about the country, preaching against the selfishness of the rich and the laziness of the clergy. During the fifteenth century many Lollards were burned to death for their beliefs.

A bonfire and a Bull

Many years passed. On a winter day in the year 1520 in the town of Wittenberg, a priest and some students of the university came into the market square bringing bundles of wood. Crowds began to gather.

'It's Luther, Martin Luther,' said one. 'Look, here he comes.'

Luther held up a paper. 'Friends and brothers,' he said, 'a message, a Bull from the Pope of Rome. This is a Bull of Excommunication. I am condemned as a heretic.'

A groan rose from the people, for this meant that Luther was cast out from the Christian Church, he could not receive God's forgiveness. Surely Luther would have to give in to the Pope, they thought. He knelt down, kindled the bonfire, and stood up. Then, raising the Pope's Bull, he threw it into the midst of the flames.

There was silence for a few moments. Then the students began to cheer. Some of the people joined in, but most did not quite know what to think. Slowly the crowd dispersed.

For some time Luther had been criticizing the Pope and the Church. He had been to Rome, and had been disgusted at the wealth and way of life of the leaders of the Church. He wrote out a long list of the things that he thought were wrong with the Church and nailed it up on the door of the church in Wittenberg. It was this which had made the Pope so angry. He was still more angry when Luther publicly burned the Bull.

New churches

Luther was ordered to leave Germany, but some of the German princes did not like the way in which

the Pope interfered in their affairs, and they protected Luther, and helped him to set up a new sort of Christian Church for the German people. This was the beginning of the Reformation. The new churches were called Lutheran or Protestant. The Bible was in German instead of Latin, and the services were simpler, so that the ordinary people could understand them, and take more part in them.

Religion in England

When news of Luther's action reached England, King Henry VIII sided with the Pope, and wrote a book against Luther. The Pope was so pleased that he gave Henry the title of Defender of the Faith. Henry was delighted, but his delight did not last for long, nor did the Pope's pleasure. Henry had been married for a long time to the Spanish princess Catherine of Aragon. He was anxious to have a son to succeed him, but no son was born, so he decided to ask the Pope to free him from his marriage with Catherine, but the Pope refused. Catherine was the aunt of the Emperor Charles V, and the Pope did not wish to offend him. Henry therefore decided to take control of Church affairs out of the hands of the Pope, and to make himself head of the Church in England. He called a Parliament to discuss it.

King instead of the Pope

Many of the Members did not like the Pope's interference in English affairs. In 1534 they passed the Act of Supremacy, which said that Henry was

Fountains Abbey, Yorkshire: a rich Cistercian Abbey built in 1132 and closed down by Henry VIII in the reformation.

the supreme head of the Church of England. Henry did not want any other changes, and people who agreed with Luther were burned to death as heretics, and so were some who thought the Pope should still be head of the Church. Sir Thomas More, a friend of the king, could not agree that anyone but the Pope should be head of the Church. He was executed as a traitor. On the scaffold he said, 'I die the King's loyal servant, but God's first.'

The monks still looked to the Pope as their head, so Henry closed all the monasteries, and monks, good and bad, were turned out. Thus Henry got rid of those who opposed him, and gained great wealth for himself and his friends from the monastery lands and riches.

Catholic or Protestant

During the reign of Edward VI there were rapid changes. Old services were discarded, and new simple Protestant ones used. But a few years later Mary became queen, and she tried to change everything back again. The Pope was once more made head of the Church in England, and now hundreds of Protestants were burned to death, including bishops and archbishops.

After five years Mary died. People were appalled by these burnings, and under Elizabeth I England became Protestant once more, and has remained so ever since.

69

Exercises and things to do

1 Write out, filling in the blanks. One – stands for each missing letter.

In the Middle Ages, all the English churches were – – – – – – – –, with the – – – – at Rome as their head. In every town and village, the church was the – – – – – – of life, and monks and – – – – – – looked after the – – – and the – – – –.

In Germany a monk named – – – – – – – – – – – – criticized the Pope, who sent him a message, or – – – – of – – – – – – – – – – – – – – –, saying that he was no longer a Christian, and that he could not receive God's forgiveness. Luther publicly – – – – – – the – – – –. He was told to leave Germany, but instead some of the German – – – – – – – helped him to set up new – – – – – – – – which had nothing to do with the – – – –, and were called – – – – – – – – or – – – – – – – – – – churches. This – – – – – – – – – – –, as it was called, spread to many other parts of Europe.

2 The heads and tails of these statements have been mixed. Write them out correctly.

(a) Henry VIII

(b) The Reformation

(c) Act of Supremacy

(d) Lollards

(e) Edward VI

(f) Protestants

(1) discontinued the Catholic church services.

(2) declared that the king was head of the Church of England.

(3) is the name given to the changes in religion.

(4) were members of the churches started by Luther.

(5) wrote a book against Luther.

(6) were English followers of Wycliffe.

Many people were tortured and executed for their religious beliefs. This picture from Foxe's book of martyrs shows three types of torture. Other people were burned, crushed or beheaded.

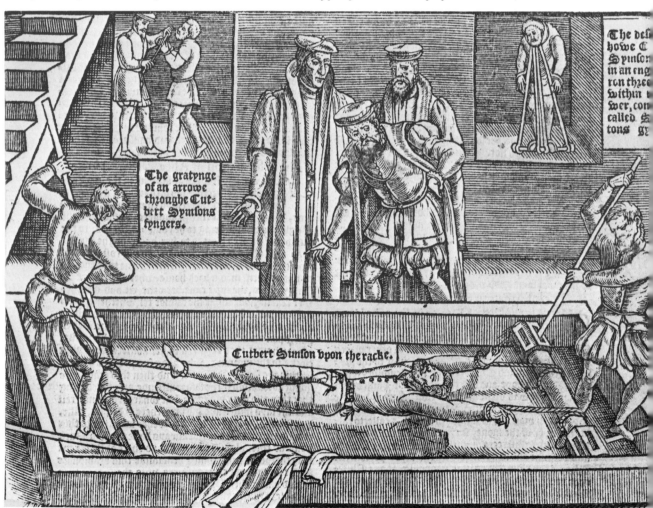

The gratynge of an arrowe throughe Cutbert Symsons fyngers.

Cutbert Simson vpon the racke.

3 *Statements of fact.* Write out the four statements in each group, in what you think is their order of importance or interest. Say in each group why you have decided to put one particular statement first.

(a) Martin Luther
  (1) criticized the Pope and the Catholic Church.
  (2) burned the Pope's Bull.
  (3) was excommunicated by the Pope.
  (4) refused to give up his beliefs.

(b) The religious changes started by Martin Luther
  (1) enabled ordinary people to understand and take part in church services.
  (2) led to the use of the language of the people in each country in their churches.
  (3) started the Reformation.
  (4) led to the setting up of Lutheran and Protestant churches.

(c) In England
  (1) Henry VIII wrote a book against Luther.
  (2) Henry VIII closed the monasteries because the monks supported the Pope.
  (3) John Wycliffe spoke against the Pope.
  (4) the Church finally broke away from the Pope and became Protestant.

4 *The right order.* Write these down in the order in which they happened.

(a) Lutheran churches were founded.
(b) England became finally Protestant in Elizabeth's reign.
(c) Luther burned the Pope's Bull.
(d) Henry VIII attacked Luther's ideas.
(e) Mary I tried to make England Catholic once more.

5 *The main idea.* Write down the one sentence which tells what you think is the main idea of this topic.

(a) Luther opposed the Pope and begged him to make changes in the Church.
(b) Luther started the Reformation which changed the history of the Church.
(c) Religion was very important in the Middle Ages.
(d) Most of the churches in England and Germany changed from Catholic to Protestant.

6 Act the scene round Luther's bonfire.

Europe after the reformation.

7 Here is a map showing the main form of Christianity in each of the countries of western Europe after the Reformation. Copy it and make a list of those which remained largely Catholic and those which became Protestant.

8 Write part of a diary which Luther might have written.

9 Write the headings 'Before the Reformation' and 'After the Reformation', and write the following statements under the correct heading. Some may go under both headings.

(a) Charles V was Emperor of Germany.
(b) Germany was mainly Catholic.
(c) France was mainly Catholic.
(d) The Pope was head of all the Christian churches in western Europe.
(e) England was a Catholic country.
(f) The Pope was head of the Church in Italy.
(g) England was a mainly Protestant country.

10 Which six people of the Middle Ages up to about 1550 dealt with in this book do you admire most, and for what reasons?

11 Are there any ways in which you think it would have been better or more interesting to have lived in the Middle Ages or the fifteenth century than today?

12 Describe what is being done to Cuthbert Simson in the three types of torture in the picture. What do you think his torturers were trying to make him do, and why?

17 The beginnings of empire: Russia and Holland

The fifteenth century saw the foundation and growth of the Portuguese and Spanish empires. The sixteenth century saw the beginnings of others, one based on the vast lands of Russia in eastern Europe and central Asia, another arising from the far-flung sea-borne trade of the small country of Holland.

Russia

Most of Russia had been over-run by the Mongols in the thirteenth century, and for two centuries had been ruled by the Mongol Golden Horde. When this broke up, Ivan the Great, Grand Duke of Moscow, saw his opportunity, and he began to extend his territory in all directions. Constantinople had fallen in 1453, and the Byzantine Empire had come to an end. Ivan the Terrible of Moscow proclaimed that Russia would take over the leadership of the Orthodox Christian Church. He took the title of Czar (Caesar or Emperor). Over a thousand years earlier Constantinople had taken the place of Rome; now Moscow was to take the place of Constantinople, and become the 'Third Rome'. Russia became known as 'Holy Russia'. The Czar sent explorers and traders to central Asia, and began to build up a great Russian Empire.

A new way to China?

Meanwhile western Europeans were trying to expand their trade with Russia. In 1553 some London merchants shared the cost of sending an expedition under Sir Hugh Willoughby and Richard Chancellor to try to find a North-east Passage to China and the East by sailing round the north of Russia and Asia. A storm separated their ships, and Willoughby was never seen alive again. But the following summer Russian fishermen found his ship at anchor. On board were the bodies of Willoughby and his crew. They had all died from starvation and cold in the Arctic winter.

Meanwhile Chancellor had wintered at the little Russian town of Archangel. Then he travelled 2400 kilometres overland to Moscow by sledge. He was surprised to find that Moscow was as big as London. The Russian people, too, surprised him. The men wore long skirted clothes; the women were shut away, and not allowed to mix with other people. The Czar ruled the land just as he wished. There was no Parliament.

A prosperous Dutch banker and his wife

The Dutch

In the sixteenth century, much of what is now Holland and Belgium was part of the Spanish Empire and known as the Spanish Netherlands. Most of the people in the north were Protestants, and lived mainly by trade; those in the south were Roman Catholics, and lived mainly by industry. They all hated being ruled by Spaniards, so they began to demand freedom and a share in the government.

The fight for freedom

Philip II of Spain decided to force the Protestants to change their religion, and become Roman Catholics. He sent the Duke of Alva to crush the people if they dared to resist. At first the north and south joined together to oppose the Spaniards. They were led by William the Silent, Prince of Orange. Time after time William was defeated, but he fought on. Dutch sailors raided Spanish

The Muscovy Company

Chancellor presented Czar Ivan the Terrible with a letter from King Edward VI, addressed to 'all Kings, Princes, Rulers, Judges and Governors of the earth in all places under the universal heaven'. The Czar agreed to open up direct trade with England, and Chancellor returned home. A Muscovy Company was formed, which bought furs, timber and naval stores in exchange for cloth.

The company sent Captain Jenkinson to Moscow in 1557, to try to penetrate into the heart of Asia, and to open up trade. He was well received by the Czar, and then sailed down the Volga and across the Caspian Sea. 'Wee set up the redde crosse of S. George in our flagges.' he wrote, 'for honour of the Christians.' He passed through various Tartar countries in a caravan of a thousand camels and reached the city of Bokhara, a 'very great city, with houses, temples and monuments of stone sumptuously builded and gilt'.

The expansion of Russia

Russia continued to grow in size and strength, and the Tartar tribes were gradually brought under Russian control. Russia was starting on the expansion which was to make her the largest country in the world, and, after the Second World War of 1939–45, one of the world's two super powers. The other, the United States of America, did not yet exist at all.

St Basil's Cathedral stands in Red Square, Moscow. It was built by Tsar Ivan the Terrible in 1555–6 to celebrate his victories over the Tartars.

shipping, and captured or destroyed Spanish treasure and supplies. They were nicknamed the Sea Beggars. In 1572 they captured the port of Brill, and held it against all attacks. The people of other towns rose and proclaimed their freedom. The Spaniards struck back. Town after town was besieged and captured, often with terrible slaughter. Thousands were killed, and many died of starvation, rather than give in. The town of Leyden held out for a whole year. At last food supplies were gone, but the people deliberately cut the dykes which kept back the sea, and the waters flooded in. The Spaniards fled, and Dutch ships sailed right to the walls with help of food for the starving people.

The Dutch Republic

In 1578 there were new Spanish attacks. The people in the south were defeated, and decided to give up the struggle, but the seven northern provinces took the name of the United Provinces, and pledged themselves never to submit to Spain. The war continued. Philip declared William a traitor. In 1584 William was murdered. Elizabeth of England sent a small army to help. War between England and Spain became certain, but the fleet of the Spanish Armada was defeated (see chapter 18), while the Dutch gained a victory over the Spanish army in Holland. In 1609 the mighty Spanish Empire was forced to agree to the independence of the Dutch Republic.

From then on, Spain gradually lost her great power. The great treasure of gold and silver she was extorting from her colonies made prices rise so high that the ordinary people were no better off. But the Dutch were now free to build up a large trading empire, with colonies in the Indies and America. England and France meanwhile joined in the competition with Spain as centres of world trade and empire.

Exercises and things to do

1 Write out, filling in the blanks. One – stands for each missing letter.

In the fifteenth century the empires of – – – – – and – – – – – – – – were growing larger. In the sixteenth century – – – – – – and – – – – – – – also began to grow stronger and build up empires. In the case of Russia, the dukes of – – – – – – steadily increased their control over more and more – – – –. In the case of Holland, while fighting to gain freedom from rule by – – – – –, the – – – – – built up their – – – – – – – –, which enabled them to defeat the – – – – – – – ships, and to make – – – – – – – stations in many parts of the world. This grew into the – – – – – Empire.

In Russia Ivan the Terrible took the title of Czar or – – – – – – –, and made Russia the leader of the Eastern – – – – – – – – – Church. Russian – – – – – – – and – – – – – – – – – were sent to open up – – – – – with central – – – –. Then the land was taken over, and became part of the growing – – – – – – – – – – – – –.

2 The heads and tails of these statements have been mixed. Write them out correctly.

(a) Richard Chancellor	(1) was the leader of the Dutch.
(b) The North-east Passage	(2) is a sea in southern Russia.
(c) Ivan the Terrible	(3) was King of Spain.
(d) William the Silent	(4) was an English explorer.
(e) Philip II	(5) was ruler of Russia.
(f) The Caspian Sea	(6) was a sea route to China.

3 *Statements of fact.* Write out the four statements in each group in what you think is their order of importance or interest. Say in each group why you have decided to put one particular statement first.

(a) In the fifteenth and sixteenth centuries
   (1) Russia was being made into a large, strong state by the princes of Moscow.
   (2) Ivan the Terrible of Russia took over the leadership of the Eastern Christian Church.
   (3) Ivan the Terrible agreed to open up trade with England.
   (4) Russia began to take over the Tartar tribes in the south-east.

(b) English merchants
   (1) sent an expedition to look for the North-east Passage to China.
   (2) founded the Muscovy Company to trade with Russia.
   (3) sent Jenkinson to see if trade could be opened up with central Asia.
   (4) exchanged English cloth for Russian furs and timber.

(c) In the sixteenth century
   (1) the people of the Netherlands were mainly Protestant in the north and Catholic in the south.
   (2) the Dutch struggled for freedom from Spanish rule.
   (3) the Spaniards tried to force the Dutch Protestants to become Catholics.
   (4) the Dutch were led by William the Silent, Prince of Orange, until he was murdered in 1584.

4 *The right order.* Write these down in the order in which they happened.

(a) Spain recognized Dutch independence.
(b) All the Netherlanders united to resist the Spaniards.
(c) William the Silent was murdered.
(d) Elizabeth sent an English army to help the Dutch.
(e) The South Netherlanders gave up the struggle against Spain.

74

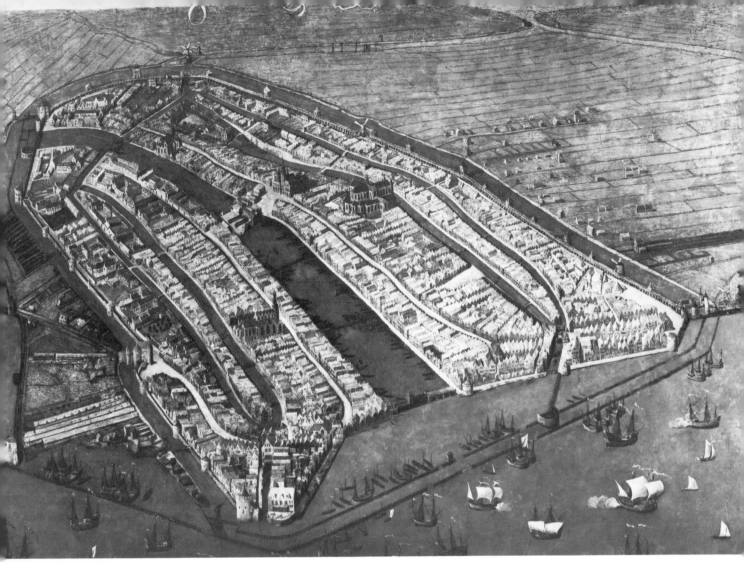

5 *The main idea.* Write down the one sentence which tells what you think is the main idea of this topic.

(a) The Spaniards failed to force the Dutch Protestants to become Catholic, and finally had to agree to their independence.
(b) The Dutch and the Russians grew in strength and trade.
(c) William the Silent led his people until they were strong enough to gain complete independence.
(d) England opened up trade with Russia, central Asia and other distant parts of the world.

6 *Thinking back.* Write out these sentences, choosing the right word from the bracket.

(a) In the late Middle Ages England's main export was (woollen cloth, coal, raw wool).
(b) The first English voyage to look for a new way to the East was led by (Columbus, Cabot, Henry the Navigator).
(c) The Russians gained their freedom from (Spanish, Mongol, Persian) rule.
(d) The English sympathized with the Dutch because under Elizabeth England was (Protestant, Roman Catholic, Moslem).

Amsterdam in the seventeenth century. The city was founded in 1275 on the Amstel River. It became the chief port and commercial centre of Holland.

(e) In the Middle Ages the trade with the East was mainly in the hands of the (English, Venetians, Portuguese).

7 The map of Russia shows how much it was growing in size. Copy it and show the journeys mentioned in this topic.

8 Imagine some of the details from the log of Willoughby's voyage which might have been found by the Russian fishermen, and write them out in diary form.

9 Why was Moscow sometimes called the 'Third Rome'?

10 Look at the picture of the Dutch banking couple on page 72. What has the painter included in the picture to show that they are rich?

11 From the drawing of Amsterdam at the top of this page, draw a map of the town. On your map show how you would get from the harbour mouth to the windmill outside the opposite end of the town (a) by road, (b) by canal.

18 The England of Elizabeth 1

A dangerous situation

There had been violent changes in religion during the reign of Edward VI when England became officially Protestant, and even more violent under Mary, when leading Protestants were burned to death. When Elizabeth became queen in 1558 the people were anxious and divided. No one knew how many Catholics there were, nor whether the Catholic kings of France or Spain might attack the country. The Pope said that Elizabeth had no right to the throne, and encouraged the Catholics to rebel against her. Mary, Queen of Scots was a Catholic, and she claimed the throne of England. The Scots actually made alliance with France. Most of the Irish were also Catholics. They had long-standing grievances against England, and were ready to welcome Spanish help in an attack on the English.

There were other difficulties in England beside religion. Under Edward VI and Mary the English navy had been neglected. Those in charge of it had sold some of the ships and kept the money for themselves. Most of the few ships left were rotten. There was no English army. King Henry VIII had started putting lead into gold coins, which had reduced their value to a quarter of what it had been. This made prices rise, which was bad for trade and for the poor. There were thousands of beggars and unemployed. This was the state of England when Queen Elizabeth I came to the throne.

A queen who cared for her people

Elizabeth was brave and strong-willed. She said, 'I care not for myself, my life is not dear to me; my care is for my people.' She made the English Church Protestant, but without the torture and burnings of people for their beliefs that was going on in many parts of Europe. She said, 'There is one faith and one Jesus Christ.' The rest to her was unimportant. She was able to inspire a united feeling of patriotism. She cleverly played off France against Spain, and avoided war until England was much stronger.

Meanwhile all the bad money was called in, and new coins of full value issued. Trade increased, and the people became more prosperous. A Poor Law was passed, and all people had to pay a poor rate to help the poor, the sick, the orphans and others who could not earn for themselves.

As England became stronger, Elizabeth was able to help the Protestant Dutch against Spain, and the Protestant Scots against the French supporters of Mary, Queen of Scots. Mary fled to England, but there she was imprisoned. Many years later, when there was a danger of a Spanish invasion, she was executed.

The English navy was rebuilt with fast, low ships with many heavy guns. They proved to be able to defeat the larger, high-built slower Spanish galleons. By the end of Elizabeth's reign England was strong and beginning to think of building an empire beyond the seas.

Sir Francis Drake

The most famous of England's sailors at that time was Francis Drake. On a trading voyage he had had to put into a Spanish harbour for repairs, when he was attacked by Spanish warships, and many of his English crew were killed. In revenge, many English sailors thought this justified any attacks they could make on Spanish treasure ships.

On one voyage Drake had landed in Central America, and he saw the Pacific. 'I will sail an English ship there before I die.' he said. In 1577 he set out with five ships, and secret instructions from the queen.

Elizabethans were fond of sports, amusements and drama. In addition to fairs and festivals there were ball games like the one in this picture, football, cricket, tennis, horse racing, bull baiting and cock fighting.

> 'This I count the glory of my crown, that I have reigned with your love. I never was a greedy scraping grasper, nor yet a waster. My heart was never set on worldly goods, but only for my subjects' good, and though you have had, and may have many mightier and wiser princes in this seat, yet you never had nor shall have any that will love you better.'

They reached the Straits of Magellan, and two of the ships were sent back. Drake passed on through the Straits. It was thought that there was a vast continent just to the south. But Drake was blown by a violent storm far to the south, and found no such continent there. After the storm, Drake's ship alone survived. He renamed it the *Golden Hind* and sailed northwards. He robbed a number of Spanish treasure ships, which were unarmed as the Spaniards looked upon it as their ocean where there was no need of defence.

Drake sailed on, past Central America, past Mexico, as far as California. He landed and, calling it New Albion, claimed it for England. Then he crossed westwards over the wide Pacific, and reached the East Indies. He took on a cargo of cloves, but then ran aground, and cloves and guns had to be thrown overboard. He continued westwards across the Indian Ocean, rounded the Cape of Good Hope, and arrived back in England after a three-year voyage. The Queen welcomed him, and knighted him aboard the *Golden Hind*.

War

For a long time Philip of Spain had avoided making war on England. But Drake's plundering of Spanish ships in the Pacific was one of the incidents that caused Philip at last to decide on war, and the conquest of Protestant England. He wanted to transport an army to England in an armada of ships. This map shows what happened.

The Armada

1 The Armada leaves Lisbon with 130 vessels and 30 000 men, July 1588.
2 Skirmishes with English ships off south coast with no advantage to either side.
3 Armada anchors off Calais. The English attack with fireships. Armada flees north.
4 Battle at sea. Some Spanish ships sunk or grounded. The rest escape northwards. English ships run out of ammunition and return to base.
5 Storms in the north of Scotland scatter Armada and wreck ships on rocks.
6 Storms force more ships onto rocks along the Irish coast.
7 The remnants of the Armada struggle home. Only 53 ships survive. Not a single soldier has been landed in England.

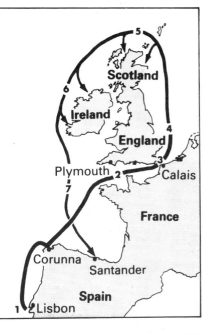

Exercises and things to do

1 Write out, filling in the blanks. One – stands for each missing letter.

At the beginning of Elizabeth's reign the people were ––––––– and afraid that the kings of –––––– and –––––, who were –––––––––, might invade –––––––, for Elizabeth had made England –––––––––– once more. She managed to avoid ––– for a long time, by ––––––– off France against –––––. Later she helped the –––––, who were ––––––––––, to fight for their freedom against –––––. She also helped the Protestants of ––––––– against the Catholic ––––, Queen of –––––.

The English navy, which had been in bad repair, was made much –––––––, with ––––, low ships, with many ––––. English sailors made many ––––––– and exploring voyages. After being attacked by ––––––– –––––––, Francis ––––– fought them whenever he could, and captured many –––––––– ships.

After that, King –––––– of ––––– sent the Spanish –––––– against England, but it was defeated.

2 The heads and tails of these statements have been mixed. Write them out correctly.

(a) Edward VI	(1) sent the Armada against England.
(b) New Albion	(2) was the name given to Drake's ship.
(c) Queen Mary of England	(3) was executed.
(d) The *Golden Hind*	(4) was the name given to California by Drake.
(e) King Philip	(5) made England officially Protestant.
(f) Mary Queen of Scots	(6) made England Catholic again.

3 *Statements of fact.* Write out the four statements in each group in what you think is their order of importance or interest. Say in each group why you have decided to put one particular statement first.

(a) Elizabeth
 (1) feared attacks from Catholic countries.
 (2) settled the religious question by making England Protestant.
 (3) played off France against Spain and avoided war for a long time.
 (4) restored the value of the coinage.

During the reign of Queen Elizabeth I, England became prosperous and strong. To show off her country's wealth, Elizabeth wore beautiful gowns of rich materials and decorated with precious stones. She wore a costume like the one in this drawing at a church service to give thanks for the defeat of the Armada.

The bodice, oversleeves and overskirt were of white satin decorated in gold. The undersleeves, stomacher and underskirt were edged with pearls, rubies and emeralds. She wore pearls hanging in her hair.

These are some of the clothes that the Queen had in her wardrobe: 99 robes; 102 French gowns; 67 round gowns; 100 loose gowns; 126 underskirts; 136 stomachers; 125 petticoats; 96 cloaks; 91 outerskirts; 43 bodices; 27 fans.

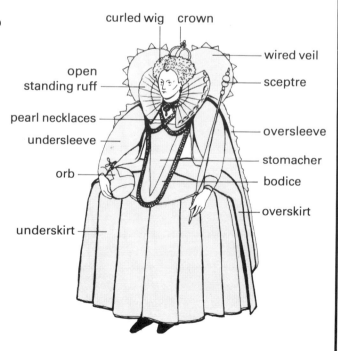

Plays were often performed in the courtyards of inns or town squares. After 1576 many theatres were built and playwrights such as Shakespeare became very famous. Musicians were hired to support the drama.

(b) The Spanish Armada
    (1) consisted of 130 ships.
    (2) was meant to land a Spanish army in England.
    (3) was scattered by English fireships.
    (4) lost more than half its ships and was a complete failure.

(c) Drake's voyage
    (1) began in 1577 and ended in 1580.
    (2) included a visit to the East Indies.
    (3) was the first time an English ship had sailed round the world.
    (4) proved that there was no great continent just south of America.

4 *The right order.* Write these down in the order in which they happened.

(a) Drake destroyed Spanish ships in his voyage round the world.
(b) Many English ships were remodelled.
(c) Elizabeth made England Protestant.
(d) The Armada was defeated.
(e) Most of the ships of the English navy were rotten.

5 *The main idea.* Write down the one sentence which tells what you think is the main idea of this topic.

(a) English seamen played a great part in making England strong in her struggle against Spain.
(b) The Armada tried to take an invading army to conquer England, but failed.
(c) Elizabeth inspired her people and overcame her difficulties, leaving England strong.
(d) Elizabeth restored the value of the coinage and so helped to keep prices down, and to improve trade.

6 Write out an imaginary part of the log of Drake's voyage round the world, basing it on the facts in the text.

7 Why do you think the English warships were able to defeat the Spanish ships?

8 Why were the Spanish treasure ships which Drake took in the Pacific unarmed?

9 Imagine that you are Francis Drake. Send a message to the Queen describing your victory over the Spanish Armada.

10 Take five different coins or medals. Place each one in turn under your paper. Shade (in pencil) over the paper until the imprint of the coin or medal shows through. Describe the design and wording on each one.

11 Copy the drawing of Queen Elizabeth on page 78. Add the details described in the box and colour your drawing to show what she really must have looked like.

12 Make a list of the main items of clothing that you own. How do they compare with Queen Elizabeth's? Why do you think she needed so many clothes?

Queen Mary (1516–58) was a devout Catholic. By marrying Philip of Spain and trying to make England Catholic, she made enemies.

19 Early colonization of North America

Sir Walter Raleigh pioneer of the empire.

One of the favourite courtiers of Elizabeth I.
He sees the potential in North America and is keen to set up a colony there.

North America

Virginia

1585
He sends an expedition to found a colony on Roanoke Island called Virginia. The colony is abandoned in 1586.

1587
Another expedition settles at Roanoke. But the colonists disappear without trace.

1595
Raleigh leads an expedition to discover El Dorado, to win South America from the Spanish and return with gold.

The expedition is a failure and he returns empty-handed.

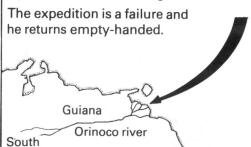

Guiana

Orinoco river

South America

1603
Elizabeth dies and James I becomes king. Raleigh does not support the king. He is sentenced to death for treason and put in prison.

1607
Meanwhile, a settlement is made in Jamestown, Virginia. At first there is great hardship, but with the profits from tobacco the colony begins to thrive.

1616
Raleigh persuades James to let him lead another expedition to Guiana to discover El Dorado. The expedition is a complete failure. Raleigh returns to England.

1618
Raleigh is beheaded for treason.

The Pilgrim Fathers

With the death of Raleigh all thought of an English empire in tropical America was given up, but other settlements were made in Virginia and further north. In 1620 a number of Puritans who were not allowed to worship as they wished in England sailed in the *Mayflower*. They founded the town of New Plymouth, in what came to be called New England. They are now known as the Pilgrim Fathers, although more than half the little band of settlers were women and children.

The French in America

Meanwhile the French had also been exploring the coast of North America. In 1534 Jacques Cartier, looking for a strait which would lead through to the Pacific, sailed along the coast. He said Labrador was 'composed of stones and horrible rugged rocks. I did not see one cartload of earth'. The next year he sailed up the St Lawrence River, and came to a region 'as fine as it is possible to see, being very fertile and covered with magnificent trees'.

In 1603 Samuel de Champlain was sent to establish a colony there, 'which should hold for France the gateway to the Golden East'. In 1608 the French colony of Quebec was founded, and in 1615 Champlain reached the Great Lakes.

The French colonists were full of zeal to convert the Indians to Christianity. Their priests travelled along the network of rivers and lakes into unknown country, while French fur traders lived among the Indians, as the Chippewa chief said, 'like brethren in the same lodge. Just, very just were they towards us.' Champlain was more fortunate than another young Frenchman named Brule, who visited Lakes Huron, Ontario and Superior, until he was killed and eaten by Indians. Champlain became involved in quarrels between Indian tribes. He was wounded, and his friends the tribe of Hurons packed him up in a basket and carried him on the back of one of their warriors. He spent the winter with the Hurons, then returned to Quebec.

An engraving showing how the North American Indians caught crocodiles

Exercises and things to do

1 Write out the following, filling in the blanks. One – stands for each missing letter.

In 1595 Raleigh led an expedition to −−−−−, hoping to take the land which was being colonized by the −−−−−−−−, but without success. Another attempt in the reign of −−−−− − also failed, and Raleigh was −−−−−−−.

The first permanent settlement in −−−−−−−− was made at −−−−−−−−− in AD −−−−. In 1620 some English −−−−−−−−, now known as the −−−−−−− −−−−−−−, built the town of −−− −−−−−−−−, and that part of −−−−−−− was called −−− −−−−−−−.

Further north the −−−−−− had been exploring and settling near the St −−−−−−−− river, and in 1608 −−−−−− was founded.

2 The heads and tails of these statements have been mixed. Write them out correctly.

(a) Roanoke	(1) was a French colony.
(b) New England	(2) was the name given to the land around Jamestown.
(c) Jamestown	(3) was settled by the Puritans.
(d) New Plymouth	(4) was founded in 1607.
(e) Quebec	(5) was an English colony.
(f) Virginia	(6) was the name of the land round New Plymouth.

3 *Statements of fact.* Write out the four statements in each group, in what you think is their order of importance or interest. Say in each group why you have decided to put one particular statement first.

(a) Sir Walter Raleigh
  (1) believed that an English empire could be built up in America.
  (2) sent a colonizing expedition to Virginia.
  (3) passed from being a royal favourite to execution as a traitor.
  (4) led an expedition to Guiana.

(b) The French
  (1) explored the coast of North America.
  (2) sailed up the St Lawrence and found the land fertile.
  (3) thought Labrador was all rocks and stones.
  (4) founded Quebec in 1608.

(c) The French explorers
  (1) hoped to find a way through America to the 'Golden East'.
  (2) were anxious to convert the Indians to Christianity.
  (3) were fur traders.
  (4) lived with the Indians as friends and brothers.

4 *The right order.* Write these down in the order in which they happened.

(a) The foundation of Jamestown.
(b) Jacques Cartier explored the American coast.
(c) Quebec was founded.
(d) The foundation of New Plymouth.
(e) The despatch of Raleigh's first party to Virginia.

5 *The main idea.* Write down the one sentence which tells what you think is the main idea of this topic.

(a) Both Britain and France wanted to found colonies in North America.
(b) Sir Walter Raleigh's dream of an English empire led to the founding of Virginia and other colonies in America.
(c) The main object of English colonists was to make their homes in America, but the French wanted to convert the people and to set up trading stations.

6 Write an account of what might have happened to the colonists on Roanoke Island. No ship had visited them for four years. Did they move to the mainland, try to build a boat to make their way back or go to live with the Indians?

7 Which of the following

(a) was visited by Raleigh
(b) was fond of him
(c) owed its existence to him
(d) was a name invented by him
(e) hated him?

Elizabeth, Guiana, James Stuart, Roanoke, Virginia.

8 Imagine you are a colonist in Jamestown. Write a letter to friends in England describing your life during the first few years.

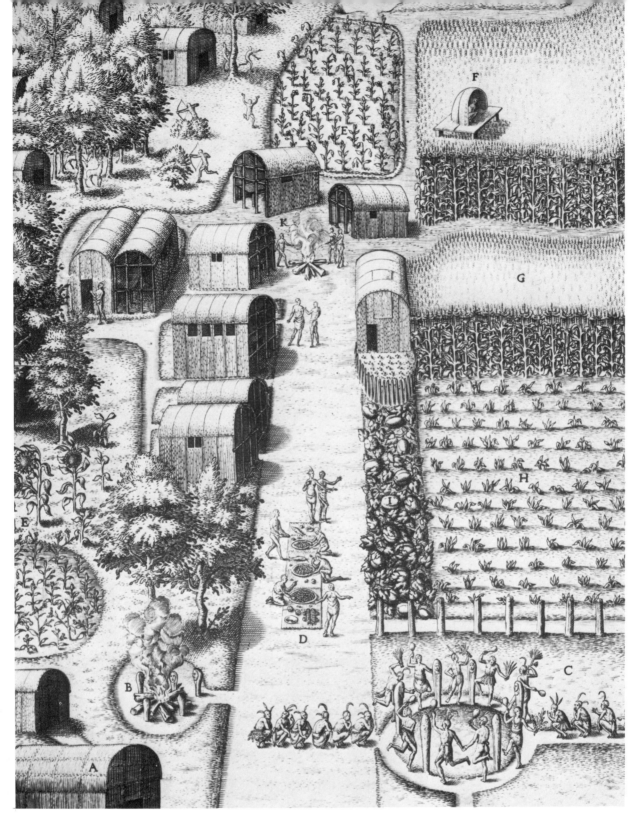

9 Look carefully at the engraving of the Indian village and read the caption.

(a) What is happening at C and at D?
(b) What is L?
(c) What is being grown beside the tobacco patch on the left? What is this crop being grown for, do you think?

10 Imagine you are John White, visiting an Indian village for the first time. Make an entry in your diary describing the things which strike you most about it.

John White was an Englishman who made many careful, detailed drawings of the Indians and their way of life. This picture and the one of the crocodile-hunting on page 81 are engravings copied from his drawings.

This drawing is of an Indian village, showing the crops they grew – tobacco (E) and pumpkins (I) – and what they did. They planted corn at different times of year to give them ripe corn all year round: H is a field of new shoots, G is the green corn and F is the ripe corn. At F, a man is crouching in a hut making noises to frighten birds and animals away from the crops. B is the place where they pray.

20 Kings and Parliament, Civil War and revolution

James I, the king by Divine Right

When Elizabeth died in 1603, the English Parliament asked her cousin James Stuart, King of Scots, to become King of England as well. He was delighted. England was much richer and more powerful than Scotland at that time, and James thought he would show the world how such a kingdom should be ruled.

James believed that he alone knew what was best for the country. He wanted to make himself like the kings of France and Spain, who had all the power in their own hands. He talked of the Divine Right of Kings, which meant that the king was ordained by God to rule just as he wished, and it was the duty of everyone to obey him. This was just at the time when the nobles, rich merchants and country gentlemen who formed Parliament were demanding a bigger share in making the laws and governing the country. He quarrelled with the House of Commons, he quarrelled with the Puritans and made hundreds of them leave the country. He upset the Catholics to such an extent that in 1605 they tried to blow him up in Parliament in the Gunpowder Plot. He quarrelled with the London merchants. He tried to rule as far as possible without Parliament.

Charles I

Charles I, who succeeded James in 1625, also believed in the Divine Right of Kings. When he asked the House of Commons to vote him certain taxes, they refused to do so until he agreed to the Petition of Right. This was a promise not to levy any taxes without their consent, and not to imprison anyone without trial. Charles did agree to the Petition, but then decided to rule without Parliament in future. For eleven years he managed to raise enough money to rule, by levying taxes which many people thought unfair and illegal. Then he tried to force the people of Scotland to use the services of the Church of England. The Scots were furious, and refused. Charles tried to raise an army to force them to obey, but his army melted away – his men sympathized with the Scots, who then marched an army into England.

Charles was forced to call a Parliament. It granted him no money, but demanded the death of Strafford, the king's chief adviser. Charles promised Strafford that no harm should come to him; but huge crowds surrounded the palace shouting for Strafford's death. Charles gave in and signed the death warrant. Parliament brought in bills limiting the king's power, and Charles agreed to everything, but secretly he was making plans to get help from abroad or from the Pope, or from army officers.

Then the members of Parliament began disputing about religion. The Puritans wanted to do away with bishops and the Prayer Book. Those who supported the Church of England thought they would rather see power in the hands of Charles than in those of the Puritans; so Charles

James I, King of England (1603–25) and Scotland

Charles I (King 1625–49) forced his opponents into civil war.

Oliver Cromwell, Parliamentarian and Lord Protector (1649–58)

was able to gather a band of supporters, called Cavaliers. Those who supported the Puritans were called Roundheads, because they cut their hair short.

Civil war

Charles tried to arrest five Puritan Members of Parliament, but they escaped. Thousands of armed men marched to London to protect their Members of Parliament. Early in 1642 Charles fled from London and began to raise an army. The Civil War had begun.

At first it looked as if the king would win. He had the army officers, and a dashing leader in Prince Rupert. But Parliament trained a 'Model Army' and their leader, Oliver Cromwell, raised his 'Ironside' cavalry. These defeated the king in 1644 at Marston Moor and in 1645 at Naseby. Charles then gave himself up to the Scots, who sold him to Parliament to hold him prisoner. From prison Charles plotted to renew the war. He persuaded the Scots to support him, and a second Civil War began. But this time Cromwell soon beat the Scots. Members who were thought to be favourable to Charles were turned out of Parliament, and the rest brought him to trial for treason against the British people. He was executed in 1649.

The Commonwealth

For eleven years there was no king, and Britain was a republic called the Commonwealth. Cromwell was made Lord Protector. He tried to rule through a Parliament, but he found it just as difficult to get on with as Charles had done, and he really depended upon the army to keep him in power.

When Cromwell died in 1658 there was no one able to take his place, and in 1660 Charles I's son Prince Charles, who for years had been in exile in Europe, was asked to become king as Charles II. He was welcomed back, and the period known as the Restoration began.

James II

The next Stuart king, James II, was a Roman Catholic. The English laws did not allow Roman Catholics to take part in government or to be officers in the army, but James declared that the king was above the law, and there was no need for the king to obey the laws of the land. He began appointing Catholics to important positions, and when Parliament called upon him to dismiss the Catholic officers, he dismissed Parliament. Then a son was born to James. The leading men in the country would not risk having another Catholic king, so in 1688 they sent a secret letter to William of Orange, the ruler of Holland, and husband of Protestant Princess Mary, asking him to bring an army to England to help drive James out. William agreed. As soon as he landed, all the leading men in James's army deserted him. There was no fighting, and James slipped away in a small boat to France.

William III

A Parliament was called, and William and Mary were made king and queen. William promised to maintain the liberties of England, and the Protestant religion. In 1689, in the Bill of Rights, he said he would not interfere with the laws of the land, but would call regular Parliaments which would decide what taxes should be raised. The 'Bloodless' or 'Glorious Revolution' was over.

Charles II (King 1660–85) – restored by Parliament

James II (King 1685–8) – Roman Catholic hated by Parliament

William and Mary (ruled 1688–1702) Protestant monarchs

Exercises and things to do

1 Write out, filling in the blanks. One – stands for each missing letter.

James ––––––, King of Scotland, became King of ––––––– in AD ––––. He believed in the Divine ––––– of –––––, which meant that a king was given his position by –––, so it was the duty of everybody to –––– the king.

   The next king, ––––––– –, tried to force the ––––– to use the –––––––– of the English ––––––, war broke out, and ––––––– had to call a –––––––––– to raise ––––– for him. Instead of doing what he wanted, Parliament put ––––––––––, the king's chief adviser, to death. Charles tried to arrest five leading –––––––, but when he failed, he left –––––– and prepared for –––.

   Oliver –––––––– became Parliament's main leader in the Civil War which followed, and he –––––––– the king's armies at ––––––– –––– and ––––––. In AD –––– Charles was ––––––––, and –––––––– became Lord ––––––––.

2 The heads and tails of these statements have been mixed. Write them out correctly.

(a) Parliament	(1) was a Protestant King of Holland.
(b) William of Orange	(2) refused to use the English Church Services.
(c) The Ironsides	(3) were supporters of King Charles.
(d) The Cavaliers	(4) were Cromwell's cavalry.
(e) The Scots	(5) quarrelled with the king about taxes.

3 *Statements of fact.* Write out the four statements in each group, in what you think is their order of importance or interest. Say in each group why you have decided to put one particular statement first.

(a) The idea of the Divine Right of Kings
   (1) enabled the king to rule as he liked.
   (2) meant that the king was appointed by God to rule the country as he thought best.
   (3) was the belief of the Stuart kings of England.
   (4) led to quarrels between king and Parliament.

Louis XIV (1638–1715). Louis became King of France in 1643 and during his reign France became one of the most powerful nations in Europe. Louis claimed absolute power over his subjects.

(b) The English Civil War
   (1) was a contest between King Charles I and Parliament.
   (2) caused Oliver Cromwell to become leader, and Lord Protector of the Commonwealth.
   (3) led to the execution of King Charles I.
   (4) lasted from 1642 to 1649.

(c) William of Orange
   (1) was a Protestant ruler of Holland.
   (2) helped the English leaders to drive out James II.
   (3) promised to rule England according to the wishes of the Protestant Parliament.
   (4) was asked by Parliament to become King of England, Wales, Scotland and Ireland and was crowned in 1688.

4 *The right order.* Write these down in the order in which they happened.

(a) Charles was defeated at Naseby.
(b) Britain became a republic.
(c) William agreed to the Bill of Rights.
(d) James II became king.
(e) James VI of Scotland became James I of England.

5 *The main idea.* Write down the one sentence which tells what you think is the main idea of this topic.

(a) Parliament won the struggle with Charles.
(b) Parliament finally won the struggle with the King when they placed William III on the throne.
(c) William III promised to maintain the liberties of the English people.
(d) The belief in the Divine Right of Kings led the English kings to quarrel with Parliament.

6 Here are nine sentences. Rearrange their order and join some of them so that the nine statements make one paragraph of four sentences. Use joining words such as 'but', 'and', 'as' and 'so', etc.

(a) The Scots invaded England.
(b) Charles was forced to call Parliament.
(c) Charles tried to force the Scots to use the English church services.
(d) Parliament did not grant Charles the money he wanted.
(e) The Scots were angry and refused.
(f) It was Parliament which decided what taxes should be levied to raise money.
(g) Charles then tried to raise an army to make them obey.
(h) Charles needed money to raise an army to drive them back.
(i) His army melted away.

7 Using an atlas and the map to the right, find out whether your town or village would have been in a Royalist or Parliamentarian area.

8 Imagine that you were a newspaper reporter. Write a story on one of the following incidents: the execution of Charles I, the return of Charles II. Give your views on the event you choose.

9 Design the front cover of a pamphlet either supporting Charles I or supporting Oliver Cromwell and Parliament.

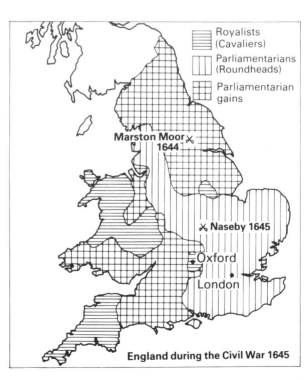

England during the Civil War 1645

21 Empire building in the Old World

After the voyages of Cabot, Columbus, da Gama, Magellan and others, Portugal, Spain, France, Holland and England found themselves at the centre of the main routes of world trade. Their ships were well placed for voyages across the Atlantic to America, round Africa to the Indies, as well as to the Baltic and the Mediterranean. There was often great rivalry between them.

The Portuguese developed a rich trade with the East Indies, but later the Dutch gained most of it for themselves. The Dutch government sent out large fleets to various parts of the world. The English, trying to increase their trade, passed Navigation Acts in 1651 to prevent goods being brought to England in Dutch ships. This caused much anger and ill feeling, and sometimes war.

India and the East

The Dutch had gained a very strong hold on the rich trade with the East Indies. In 1623 they were able to prevent the English traders from establishing themselves there at all. The English then turned to developing trade with the mainland of India. When the Portuguese tried to drive them out, they completely defeated a Portuguese fleet, and set up English trading stations, or 'factories' as they were called. At Surat the English traders formed a 'Little England', where everything was done in English fashion – English clothes, English food, English church services. At Agra, the English adopted Indian customs, wearing turbans and other Indian dress, sitting on the floor for meals, and eating Indian food.

Louis XIV and war in Europe

The French were also interested in India, and King Louis XIV encouraged colonizing and trading companies. But he was more interested in making France the strongest country in Europe, and was often at war with Holland, Austria and the states of Germany. He therefore had less money and fewer soldiers to spare for empire-building in India. Louis XIV was a Roman Catholic, and he tried to make all French people Catholic too. Hundreds of thousands of Protestants were shut away in prisons for the sake of their religion. Many skilful craftworkers fled from France, and took their skill to England, Holland and Germany, and became valuable citizens there.

Louis tried to over-run Holland. When the Dutch William of Orange became King of England, William was glad to have Britain's help in the struggle of Holland against France. After Blenheim and several other victories Britain and her allies forced Louis to make peace, and Holland's freedom was safe.

English and French in India

During the war, Britain's overseas trade had prospered while much French merchant shipping was destroyed. Britain's trading stations in India, set

Peter the Great of Russia

Meanwhile another European ruler was building up his country's strength and founding another empire. Under the Czar Peter the Great, Russia was for the first time thrusting her way into the affairs of western Europe. He was determined to make his country strong, and was most anxious to gain better outlets to the sea for Russian shipping. Sweden at that time ruled the eastern shores of the Baltic Sea, so Russia's only port to the west was Archangel, which was frozen for half the year.

Peter showed great interest in life and customs in western Europe. He himself travelled there, and worked in Dutch and English shipyards. When he returned, he was determined to make his people live like the Europeans, despite the strength of Russian traditions. He cut off the beards and moustaches of his leading men and made them wear western clothes, to their horror. He decided to build a new capital city on the Baltic, facing west. St Petersburg was founded in 1702 on desolate marshy land recently conquered from Sweden. Thousands of peasants died in the work of draining the marshes and laying foundations. Twenty years later it was the largest city in northern Europe. Russia had become a great European power.

The Russian Empire

Russia was also building an empire, not of overseas colonies, but of the vast land of Siberia. For a long time hunters and trappers had been making

up by the East India Company, were growing in strength. But in the eighteenth century the French also gave increasing attention to India, and intense rivalry grew up between them. A clever Frenchman, Dupleix, used the quarrels between native Indian princes to increase French influence. He armed the followers of certain princes and so helped them to gain power. In return he hoped to gain most of the Indian trade for France, and even to drive out the British altogether. But

A well-dressed European tea planter supervises Indians on a tea plantation. The Dutch brought tea to Europe but the French and British were trading rivals.

an equally clever Englishman, Robert Clive, played him at his own game and beat him. A huge area of India came under the rule of the East India Company. Gradually district after district was taken over by the British until they controlled most of India, while French trade was undermined on all sides.

their way through the great forests, which teemed with fur-bearing animals. They overcame the small tribes who wandered over these vast areas. Settlements surrounded with timber stockades were made, and there the native people brought furs to buy peace from their conquerors. When a settlement was accepted, that area was taken over by the government, and soldiers, monks and priests moved in to persuade the native people who had their own customs to accept the Russian religion and way of life. In the seventeenth century the Pacific was reached. Russia had become a world power.

To make his men look like Europeans, Peter the Great forced them to cut off their beards and moustaches.

89

Exercises and things to do

1 Write out, filling in the blanks. One – stands for each missing letter.

The great voyages of discovery meant that the western – – – – – – – countries found themselves in the – – – – – – of the world – – – – – – – – – –. There was rivalry between them, particularly between the – – – – –, – – – – – –, – – – – – – –, and – – – – – – – – – –.

   In India the English drove out most of the – – – – – – – – – –, and set up trading – – – – – – – – or – – – – – – – – –. Then the French, led by – – – – – – –, began to build up their power and – – – – –. In exchange for the right to trade, he helped certain – – – – – – princes to gain power by giving them – – – –; but Robert – – – – – defeated Dupleix's Indian princes and – – – – – – – and so a great deal of the land of – – – – – came under English control, while – – – – – – trade there was threatened.

2 The heads and tails of these statements have been mixed. Write them out correctly.

(a) The Dutch	(1) were England's main rivals in India.
(b) Dupleix	(2) was Russia's only port open to the West.
(c) The French	(3) were prevented from trading with the Indies by the Dutch.
(d) Peter the Great	(4) was the leader of the French in India.
(e) Archangel	(5) wanted to include Siberia in the empire he was building.
(f) The English	(6) at first gained most of the East Indies trade from the Portuguese.

An eighteenth-century print showing rich ladies drinking tea. It was a fashionable but expensive drink. Those who could afford to buy it often locked it in tea caddies.

3 *Statements of fact.* Write out the four statements in each group in what you think is their order of importance or interest. Say in each group why you have decided to put one particular statement first.

(a) In western Europe
  (1) Louis XIV tried to make all the French people Catholic.
  (2) Britain passed Navigation Acts to stop Dutch ships bringing goods to Britain.
  (3) Britain and other countries were in a good position for trade, being at the centre of world trade routes.
  (4) Louis XIV tried to make France the strongest country in Europe.

(b) The Dutch
  (1) sent out large trading fleets.
  (2) seized the trade in spices from the Portuguese.
  (3) prevented English traders from trading with the East Indies.
  (4) were angered by British Navigation Acts which excluded their ships from British ports, and this led to war.

(c) Peter the Great
  (1) served as a workman in English and Dutch shipyards.
  (2) tried to gain better outlets for Russian shipping.
  (3) visited several countries to find out about western Europe.
  (4) gained land from Sweden and built a new capital city of St Petersburg.

4 *The right order.* Write these down in the order in which they happened.

(a) England and Holland became allies under William of Orange.

(b) Dupleix planned to drive the British from India.
(c) Peter the Great founded St Petersburg.
(d) The English passed the Navigation Acts.

5 *The main idea.* Write down the one sentence which tells what you think is the main idea of this topic.

(a) While empires based on sea-borne trade were being built up by Holland and Britain, France was expanding her power in Europe and Russia was creating a land empire.
(b) England and Holland were great trade rivals.
(c) During the seventeenth and much of the eighteenth centuries there was much empire-building.
(d) Britain and France were rivals for trade and control in India.

6 From the map find out what possible outlets to the open sea Russia could hope to obtain. What drawbacks would there be in each case?

7 Why did Peter the Great wish to make Russia like European countries?

8 Look at the picture of the ladies drinking tea. Describe what you can see in the picture, including the furniture, decorations and ornaments.

9 Look in your kitchen or pantry and make a list of 20 types of food which come from other countries.

10 Using other books write a short biography of Clive of India. You may illustrate your biography.

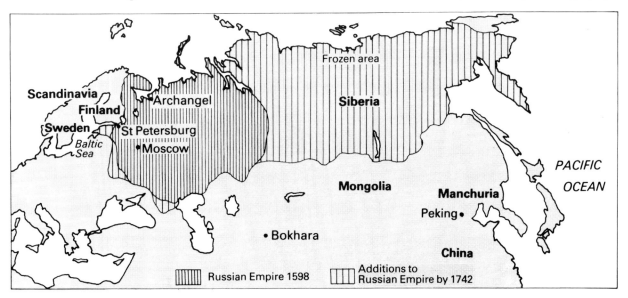

Scandinavia
Finland
Sweden
Baltic Sea
Archangel
St Petersburg
• Moscow
Frozen area
Siberia
Mongolia
Manchuria
Peking •
• Bokhara
China
PACIFIC OCEAN

⫼ Russian Empire 1598 ⫼ Additions to Russian Empire by 1742

22 Empire building in the New World: the birth of the United States of America

British colonists in North America

A number of people left Britain in the eighteenth century, either because they were not paid enough to live or because their religion was not tolerated. Many of them sailed for North America and made homes for themselves in a 'New England' across the sea. All along the Atlantic coastlands, from Florida to Nova Scotia, settlements were made.

The French in North America

The French had settled along the St Lawrence river and near the Great Lakes. Then they had sailed down the Mississippi to the Gulf of Mexico, claiming all the land along its course for France, thus cutting off the British colonies from the chance of expanding westwards across America to the Pacific. A line of French forts was built to hem in the British.

Many of the French in America were fur traders, hunters and trappers, and they made friends with the Indians, who lived the same kind of life. They often shared camps. The British, however, had taken large areas of Indian land, and made their homes and plantations there. When trouble arose between the British and French, therefore, most of the Indians sided with the French.

English v. French

Most of the British colonists were not anxious to fight the French, so long as they were left alone. But the two nations were at war in Europe, so Britain sent out troops to America to fight the French. At first the British troops, moving in columns, in bright red uniforms, formed an easy target, and ambushed and shot down by the French and Indians. Then William Pitt, the Prime Minister, planned a great campaign in North America under the command of James Wolfe. A surprise attack led to the capture of Quebec, the main French stronghold, in 1759. Both sides waited anxiously for reinforcements from Europe. Britain had control of the sea, so it was British ships which sailed up the St Lawrence. All French resistance in North America ended in 1760 with the fall of Montreal.

Meanwhile France had spent most of her resources in fighting the Prussians in Europe, and Pitt had been supplying the Prussians with arms and money. When the war in Europe ended with the Peace of Paris in 1763, the ownership of American territories was included in the treaty. The whole of Canada, Louisiana and Florida passed to Britain. Pitt said that he had 'conquered America on the plains of Germany'. But no sooner had Britain gained control of most of North America than she lost the greater part of it again. There was civil war in the British Empire.

The USA

The defence of the colonies had cost a great deal, and the government in Britain thought it only fair that the colonists in America should pay something towards it.

In 1765 the Parliament in Britain passed the Stamp Act, making the colonists pay for a stamp on all business agreements. The colonists were very angry. British people had long maintained that the only taxes they ought to pay were those that their Members of Parliament had agreed to, but there were no colonists represented in the

British Parliament. The colonists said that the Parliament in Britain was not their Parliament; it had therefore no right to force them to pay taxes they had not agreed to.

The colonists unite

The thirteen colonies were very different from one another. Each colony had its own charter and some kind of assembly or local parliament. Each colony was jealous of its own rights, and even when attacked by the Indians and French, they had found it very difficult to work together. Now, however, anger at taxation did what fear of enemies could not do – they began to unite. A congress was called, and nine of the thirteen met. They raised the slogan 'No taxation without representation', and all agreed to refuse to use the stamps.

There was a change of government in Britain at that point, and the Stamp Act was repealed. But a few years later the British government put a tax on all tea, glass and paper going into the colonies. There was immediate resistance. Stones were thrown at soldiers supporting the customs officers. The soldiers fired and killed four colonists. At Boston other colonists disguised as Indians threw 340 chests of tea into the harbour, in the incident known as the 'Boston Tea Party'. Britain closed the port of Boston and took away its charter.

The War of Independence

In 1774 delegates from twelve colonies met at Philadelphia and agreed to break off all trade with Britain. The next year the War of Independence

General James Wolfe (1727–59) led the successful English attack against the French-held city of Quebec in 1759.

began, and George Washington was appointed commander of the army of all the colonies. On 4 July 1776 the Declaration of Independence was signed – they no longer considered themselves to be colonies, but one independent country.

The British attacked the middle colonies. Washington was defeated, and New York fell. In 1777 a British army under General Burgoyne was surrounded in the wooded hills to the north, and forced to surrender at Saratoga. But another British army had taken Philadelphia, and Washington was defeated in two battles near the town. Nevertheless, Saratoga proved to be the turning point of the war. When the news of Burgoyne's surrender reached Paris, France decided to help the colonists. Troops and supplies were sent to Washington's aid. Spain and Holland entered the war against Britain. The British navy was outnumbered, and reinforcements could not be brought to the British army under Cornwallis in Virginia. Instead, a French fleet appeared off the coast, while Washington linked up with a French force and attacked by land. In 1781 Cornwallis surrendered. The war was over. The richest and most populous part of the British Empire had become the United States of America.

This was one of the most important events in history. The USA was going to take an increasingly important part in world affairs. In fact, the second of the two super powers of the twentieth century had been born.

93

Exercises and things to do

1 Write out, filling in the blanks. One – stands for each missing letter.

When Britain and France were at ––– in ––––––, the fighting spread to the ––––––––, and British –––––– were sent to defend the –––––––––. The French were beaten, and most of the French areas came under ––––––– control. The British –––––––––– thought it only fair that the colonists should help to ––– part of the –––– of the war, and put on certain –––––. The colonists said that as there were no colonists in the –––––– Parliament, the British had no right to force them to pay ––––– they had not –––––– to. The ––– of –––––––– –––––––––––– started. France helped the colonists, and the British –––––– were forced to ––––––––––. Thus the United –––––– of ––––––– came into existence.

2 The heads and tails of these statements have been mixed. Write them out correctly.

(a) William Pitt
(b) The capture of Montreal
(c) James Wolfe
(d) George Washington
(e) The surrender at Saratoga
(f) Cornwallis

(1) surrendered in Virginia.
(2) encouraged the French to help the colonists.
(3) was leader of the British colonists' army.
(4) led the English in the capture of Quebec.
(5) ended French resistance in North America.
(6) was the British Prime Minister.

3 *Statements of fact.* Write out the four statements in each group, in what you think is their order of importance or interest. Say in each group why you have decided to put one particular statement first.

(a) The British government
  (1) decided to make the colonists pay part of the cost of their defence.
  (2) passed the Stamp Act which was a kind of tax on the colonists.
  (3) put a tax on tea, glass and paper.
  (4) closed the port of Boston and prepared for war.

(b) The colonists
  (1) united, in spite of differences, to resist what they thought was unfair taxation.
  (2) were very different from one another.
  (3) said 'No taxation without representation'.
  (4) were jealous of their rights.

(c) In the War of American Independence
  (1) George Washington led the colonists.
  (2) the British under Cornwallis surrendered.
  (3) the French helped the colonists.
  (4) the colonists under Washington won with French help.

4 *The right order.* Write these down in the order in which they happened.

(a) The Declaration of Independence.
(b) Cornwallis surrendered.
(c) Taxes were put on tea.
(d) Most of Canada became British.
(e) The British captured Quebec.

5 *The main idea.* Write down the one sentence which tells what you think is the main idea of this topic.

(a) The British colonists of North America fought for and won their independence.
(b) The British government tried to tax the colonists.
(c) The French helped the colonists to win the war.
(d) The colonists, though very different, united to resist taxation and to fight Britain.

6 *Thinking back.* Write out these sentences, choosing the right word from the bracket, if possible without looking back at previous topics.

(a) The English Civil War started in (1603, 1642, 1649).
(b) The first Englishman to try to start a colony in North America was (Drake, Raleigh, James I).
(c) New England was founded in (1585, 1607, 1620).
(d) Most of South America was colonized by (Spain, France, Holland).

7 Some members of the British Parliament, including William Pitt, were against sending troops to force the colonists to submit. Write a speech one of them might have made in Parliament, and then a reply that might have been made by a supporter of the government.

8 Here are the flags of the USA, just after the War of Independence and today. What do you think the number of stars represents?

9 Here is part of the Declaration of Independence. Write it out filling in the blanks with these words: all, Creator, equal, happiness, honour, liberty, lives, rights, truths.

'We hold these —————— to be self-evident: that ——— men are created —————; that they are endowed by their —————— with certain inalienable —————; that among these are life, —————— and the pursuit of ——————————. We mutually pledge to each other our —————, our fortunes and our sacred ——————.'

'Freedom' and 'liberty' were words used by the American colonists in their fight against British rule. American liberty is here shown as a young woman holding the U.S. flag and bringing together old and new people of the country.

10 Look carefully at the picture of American liberty. Who do you think are represented by the children? Why are they shown as children, do you think?

The men painted on the pillar are Christopher Columbus, Amerigo Vespucci, Walter Raleigh, Benjamin Franklin, George Washington and Thomas Jefferson. Find out about any you don't know about and then say why you think each man has been included in this picture of America as a new, young country.

11 Some events which may not have appeared very important in themselves prove to have been turning points in history, and have led to great changes. Select six events dealt with in this book which you think were the most important turning points, and say why you think they were important.

Index